LIBER ANGELORUM
THE BOOK OF THE ANGELS

LIBER ANGELORUM

THE BOOK OF THE ANGELS

BEING AN INSTRUCTION
OF THE OFFICE
OF THE 360 ANGELS OF THE ZODIAC

Gary St. M. Nottingham

Published by Avalonia
www.avaloniabooks.co.uk

Published by Avalonia
BM Avalonia, London, WC1N 3XX, England, UK
www.avaloniabooks.co.uk

LIBER ANGELORUM – The Book of the Angels
© Gary. St. M. Nottingham, 2018
All rights reserved.

First Paperback Edition, Published by Avalonia, September 2019
ISBN 978-1-910191-16-3 (PB)

Typeset and design by Satori

Photographs and artwork by Frances Nottingham and Gary St. M. Nottingham.

British Library Cataloguing in Publication Data. A catalogue record for this book is available from the British Library.

The information provided in this book hopes to inspire and inform. The author and publisher assumes no responsibility for the effects, or lack thereof, obtained from the practices described in this book.

This book is sold subject to the condition that no part of it may be reproduced or utilized in any form or by any means, electronic or mechanical, including photocopying, microfilm, recording, or by any information storage and retrieval system, or used in another book, without written permission from the author.

About the Author

Gary St. M. Nottingham first came across alchemy when he was fifteen through reading the popular early 1970's occult magazine *'Man, Myth & Magic.'*

This encouraged him to find out further about the arte and to study Israel Regardie's 'The Philosopher's Stone'; this in turn led to the works of Hollandus, Paracelsus and eventually Junius. However, it was his involvement with a group of alchemical practitioners that opened many of the doors for him and much that he had learnt finally began to make sense.

Subsequently he has taught and written extensively on the alchemical arte, running several one-day workshops and weekends on practical laboratory alchemy.

His other areas of occult study are astrology, grimoires, and the Kabbalah, all of which are expressed as part of his alchemical work.

Table of Contents

Introduction to the Ars Paulina By David Cypher 10
    HISTORY 10
    A NOTE ON THE SIGILS: 14
    SOME PERSONAL NOTES ON HOW I APPROACHED THIS WORK 15

THE STAGE IS SET 19

THE TWELVE TRIBES OF THE ZODIAC 22
    ARIES 22
        Invocation of Aries 22
        Of the Angels of Aries and Their Seals: 23
    TAURUS 33
        Invocation of Taurus… 33
        Of the Angels of Taurus… 34
    GEMINI 44
        Invocation of Gemini… 44
        Angels of Gemini 45
    CANCER 55
        Invocation of Cancer… 55
        Angels of Cancer… 56
    LEO 66
        Invocation of Leo… 66
        Angels of Leo… 67
    VIRGO 77
        Invocation of Virgo… 77
        Angels of Virgo… 78
    LIBRA 88
        Invocation of Libra 88
        Angels of Libra… 89
    SCORPIO 99
        Invocation of Scorpio… 99
        Angels of Scorpio… 100

SAGITTARIUS	110
Invocation of Sagittarius...	*110*
Angels of Sagittarius	*111*
CAPRICORN	121
Invocation of Capricorn...	*121*
Angels of Capricorn	*122*
AQUARIUS	132
Invocation of Aquarius...	*132*
Angels of Aquarius	*133*
PISCES	143
Invocation of Pisces...	*143*
Angels of Pisces	*144*
PRAXIS	**154**
WORKING WITH THE ZODIAC	154
THE ANGELS OF THE ZODIAC	155
MEDITATION	156
PATHWORKING	156
CANDLE MAGIC	157
CONJURATION	157
TALISMANS	158
RITUALS	158
Pathworking	*158*
Candle Magic Ritual	*160*
Talismans	*161*
INDEX	**167**

For Mary.

Introduction to the Ars Paulina
By David Cypher

I have been lucky to have had an advance preview of the material that constitutes this book, and have also had the pleasure of working with it for the last year. In this introduction, I plan to briefly set out the origins of this exciting grimoire, and in doing so emphasise both its practical use and its importance for today's occultist. I will be directing the reader to explore Ars Angelorum as the clearest and operable form of this grimoire, discussing along the way why this is the case, and setting out the techniques that have led to the development of this book.

Before I go any further, let me set out what the Pauline Arte actually is. It is a catalogue of 360 spirits ruled over by a series of archangels and angels, who are both assigned and divided up within the 12 signs of the zodiac. This means that with some simple astrology, the magician can cast, or have cast, their birth chart, and in the process, they will discover the degrees of the starting points of each of the houses in their natal chart. To each of these degrees are assigned an angel, one of the 360 angels previously referred to. This means that every area of the magician's life, as set out in their natal chart, is ruled by an angel and an archangel, who are governed by a variant of the Divine Name Tetragrammaton which will also govern the sign in question. The grimoire can form an initiatory process into self-discovery, and also place the magician in contact with those angels who influence various aspects of one's life.

History

In truth, it is very difficult to pin down the history of the Ars Paulina (*Pauline Art*) exactly. But there are glimmers of interest that help us to untangle the magical technology of this most fascinating book; streamlining its practices into efficiency.

The best place to begin our journey is with the English occultist and translator Robert Turner (1619-64), who was responsible for translating a number of grimoires such as:

1: De Heptarchia

2: The Book of Treasure Spirits

3: The Arbatel of Magic

4: Ars Notoria

5: The Archidoxes of Magic

And most importantly for us today, *The Lesser Key of Solomon*, which included the Pauline Art.

In translating the Pauline Art, Turner was drawing on the works of Paracelsus (in particular his *Archidoxes of Magic*), Elias Ashmole and Dr John Dee.

During the 1640s, despite the English civil war, various members of the occult intelligentsia regularly met at the White Hart, London, where they discussed astrology and magic. The politics of the day were laid aside as those attending often held opposing views.

The flood of occult knowledge into England was partly due to the occult interests of the Medici family who had various occult works translated, which in time found their way into the corpus of the Rosicrucian current. With war and persecution, many individuals from the continent found their way to England, bringing such works with them as they fled.

The mythology of the Pauline Art, as set out in the second book of Steganographia, written by Johannes Trithemius, is attributed to St Paul, hence the name.

Turner utilises Paracelsus' Archidoxes of Magic as a source to describe each sign of the zodiac, a knowledge of which is useful for the Pauline Art. Despite the best efforts of Turner, the translation, although faithful to the Pauline Art, leaves us with a clunky grimoire, with a typically Christian approach to the traditional magic within. This is in turn word heavy, prayerful and empowered with long conjurations. The hierarchy, explained by authors both in history and in recent times, have merely included the grimoire in the Lesser Key of Solomon, but have not disclosed its actual use.

It has been pointed out to me that the conjurations in the Pauline Art have been taken from the Theurgia Goetia, as a means to operate this grimoire. The Theurgia Goetia is heavily influenced by the Steganographia, which as previously stated was a book used to clarify the Pauline Art. With this in mind, we must consider Trithemius as one of the key figures in the magic of the Middle Ages.

Trithemius is the lynchpin of the enrichment of the occult culture in Europe, and it is through his works and understanding on magic that we have a more eloquent and refined approach to this grimoire, as set down in this work.

Johann Von Heidenberg was born 1st February 1462, and the name Trithemius refers to his birthplace Trittenheim. His father died when he was a child, and after his mother's re-marriage, to a man who opposed his education, he left and travelled to Trier, Cologne and Heidelberg. On completing his studies at the university in 1482, he was travelling back home when he was caught in a snowstorm and took refuge in the nearby Benedictine abbey of Sponheim. Becoming attracted to monastic life, he decided to become a member of the community and later, at 21, he was elected abbot.

During this time he expanded the abbey's library from 50 books to 2000. After having had his appetite for the occult whetted at Heidelburg, he instructed his agents to acquire works of interest during their travels in Europe.

His reputation as a learned man and philosopher widened beyond his locality, and his fame became a double-edged sword. His reputation attracted the best and brightest minds of the day to the abbey. For this reason, both Agrippa and Paracelsus found their way to him.

However, the downside is that he acquired a reputation of having invented certain historical events. Why this is so, I do not know, because the majority of his historical works are excellent.

The other element that tarnished his meteoric rise to prominence was his skill and reputation as a magician. In 1506 Trithemius was forced to resign as abbot of Sponheim, but he soon found another position as abbot at the abbey of St James in Wurzburg, by invitation of the local bishop. He remained there until his death in December 1516.

I would argue that much of Trithemius' occult knowledge wasn't written down until his student Heinrich Cornelius Agrippa Von Nettesheim organised that material into his famous 'Three Books of Occult Philosophy.' Agrippa (1486-1535) was a son of a minor Austrian noble. He became an accomplished soldier, physician, lawyer and theologian. Although he was deemed to be an able soldier, his ambition was to be a scholar and theologian, an ambition which he achieved for a short while until his wife died. At this point, his life seemed to have fallen apart, and he had to leave his position, something he lamented for the rest of his life.

Curiously, if he hadn't pursued the publication of 'The Three Books of Occult Philosophy,' he would have acted as Catherine of Aragon's lawyer in her divorce from Henry VIII. He had been sent for and arrived in London to assist her, but her advisers, on becoming aware of the imminent publication of his occult work, considered that it would be too detrimental for her to be known to have associated with him. They paid him for his three months stay in London, but his services were not required.

Prior to the age of mass communication, Agrippa was in contact with other occultists in Europe and was instrumental in mentoring small groups of occult students. His system of magic is an amalgamation of Greek and Roman occult thinking, with its roots in Apuleius, Pliny the Elder, Ovid, Virgil and Hermes Trismegistus. Agrippa also drew upon the works of Ficino, the Kabbalah and Neoplatonism. He was further influenced by the works of Reuchlin and Pico della Mirandola. Undoubtedly all this was possible due to the expansion of the library under Abbot Trithemius, who was also influential in the teaching of Theophrastus Bombastus Von Hohenheim, better known as Paracelsus (1493-1541), who was born in Zurich. Paracelsus was the son of a physician and during his lifetime gained an impressive knowledge of alchemy, astrology, magic and medicine.

Using the works of both these authors, we can approach the Ars Paulina and make a successful working, based upon the lore to be found within the 'Three Books of Occult Philosophy.' Due to the varied sources which influenced 'The Three Books', Agrippa was able to create formulae of operation. The simple formula is that each part of creation is under the dominion of one of the seven classical planets, with each having the following:

- God name
- Archangel
- Angel
- Intelligence
- Spirit

This simple formula, with its roots in antiquity, enabled a streamlined method of communication with any group of spirits. It also meant Agrippa, Paracelsus and their students could modernise confusing ancient texts making them operable.

The final element that has been woven into this work is the imagery of Charubel (1826-1909), who like John Thomas was a Methodist minister from Montgomery in mid-Wales. He was particulary noted for his ability to heal with occult means - which brought him into conflict with the chapel authorities. He subsequently left and created an occult group, also writing an astrological work 'The Degrees of the Zodiac Symbolised' in which he drew upon Johannes Angelus' 'Astrological Optics', which had been first published in 1655. It is these texts which I have drawn upon to form the meditative imagery for each degree of the zodiac.

I must point out that there has been a trend in recent years among grimoire traditionalists to slavishly follow the instructions in grimoires down to the last letter and stick to the minutiae of the written word. However, the grimoire tradition is rather one of following basic rules and then improvising the material to bring it up to date in the era in which it is being practiced; the material in this book follows such an approach. One you know the laws of magic - the rules that cannot be broken - you can operate within those boundaries, which themselves provide quite a degree of flexibility.

A note on the sigils:

The sigils for each angel used throughout the book were generated by writing out the numbers 1-9 and then placing the letters of the alphabet below each number.

1	2	3	4	5	6	7	8	9
A	B	C	D	E	F	G	H	I
J	K	L	M	N	O	P	Q	R
S	T	U	V	W	X	Y	Z	

This allowed the expediency of being able to compose the sigil of each angel on the relevant planetary kamea (planetary square). By changing the letters of the angel's name into numbers from the grid, the numbers can then be traced on the planetary square. For example, the angels of Taurus and Libra, who are ruled by Venus, have their sigils drawn on the Venus kamea. The magical advantage to this approach is that not only is this traditional (from the point of view of utilising a technique found within the 'Three Books...' but it gives the magician a clear and untainted 'phone number' for each angel, one which is easy to draw and free from a cumbersome composition.

Some personal notes on how I approached this work

What follows is my methodology and some of my discoveries, that may be applicable to a broader audience. This section may serve as a 'how not to' go about the work for some, or it may inspire others to copy or modify my approach. I must emphasise that my approach is not set in stone and my discoveries may not be universal or indeed applicable to you.

My approach is summed up thus:
1. Perform a zone rite, to cleanse and prepare the temple/workspace and the magician. It also calls out to the subtle levels that something of note is about to happen.

    Many magicians will use the Lesser Banishing Ritual of the Pentagram (LBRP), magical technology from the 19th century popularised by the Golden Dawn. Personally, however, I do not use this for any workings these days: I used to back in my early days, but I quickly discovered (for me) that it made magic an uphill struggle. It somehow worked too thoroughly to clean the temple, acting like psychic bleach, and all spiritual contact was 'over-cleansed,' making it very difficult for even the desired spirit to lend assistance. It also seemed to short-out the magic itself.

    The second reason why I do not use the LBRP is because I have read (and more importantly, used) The Golden Dawn by Regardie, which I have discovered is rarely done. In this book Regardie stipulates that the LBRP was used as a training tool and was not used in magic beyond a certain grade. It was designed, in fact, simply to awaken the student to the concept of the spirit world being real! This is, in my opinion, why the magic shorts-out - because the energy raised, along with the magician's, help feed the phenomenon experienced, rather than going to any magical target. Most magicians I know (ones who actually practice and don't just collect books and go to occult events), if they use the LBRP, have in fact altered it in some way for their personal use, making it operable. The choice is yours. Magic is a ceremonial art form to be used as you see fit. For what it is worth, I use the 7 vowels from the Greek Magical Papyri, which connect with the 7 classical planets and their sacred directions.

The sense of protection and alignment come from practicing the Middle Pillar.
2. Light appropriate incense. This sets the vibrational rate for the ritual. It is also used as a spiritual currency to pay the spirit for its efforts.
3. Perform The Middle Pillar (the only piece of Golden Dawn tech I currently use), or similar energy-raising method. Finish with a suitable planetary colour.
4. Anoint and light the candle. This helps increase connection to the angel and allows the spirit to have a foothold on this reality whilst communication is happening. It also acts as a kind of fuel/payment for the spirit.
5. Intone the names associated with the ruling sign.
6. Perform the invocation for the sign.
7. Visualise the associated imagery over the candle flame.
8. Call the angel through the candle flame. See the candle flame as a bridge to its realm.
9. Meditation and communion. A divination tool may be used here.
10. Offerings (more incense) and thanks.
11. License to depart.
12. A fire bowl with appropriate psalm recited to close the operation down.

All rituals should happen in the appropriate planetary hour for the sign which governs the angel.

A suggested way to work with the material is to wait until the moon is in the sign and of the degree of the sign that the angel that you wish to work with rules. Another approach, one that I have been working with, is to wait until the Sun travels over the degree that the angel you want to work with rules, and work with them then. This will then become an operation taking a year to complete, one of initiation and self-discovery. It is a good idea to complete one approach and then try another. Start with your first house angel, this angel is considered to be your lesser guardian angel, and will help illuminate your contact with the other 11 personal angels of your birth chart who rule over the various aspects of your life.

I would strongly suggest a whole cycle of contact before you ask the angels to intercede in your worldly or personal matters.

When I reached number 9 in the list, I employed a light trance and the Lenormand tarot cards, using 3 cards to answer the questions I wanted the spirit to advise me on. I am a competent scryer, and know my way around a tarot deck, which is why I chose for this operation a system of divination I knew little about and had even less experience of. Due to wanting to do long-term work with these angels, I wanted to make sure (as far as is ever possible), that I was not dressed up in my spare bedroom talking to myself! The outcome of the cards was recorded in my magical diary and interpreted after the ritual. The readings were staggering! Every time an angel has answered through the cards, they answered with appropriate responses to their office and have given insight into events and questions.

Below is a list of questions that I have asked every angel in the cycle:

1. Is this oracle a suitable way to contact you?
2. What is the nature of your office?
3. How do you work with me?
4. How can I work better with you?
5. What impact are you having on (insert day, month or year etc, in question)?
6. Can you be worked with to increase/decrease...?
7. Do you have an impact on ancestral obligation?
8. How are you affected by Mars (or one of the other planets etc) transiting your house?
9. Will you come again when called?

Some angels have responded by saying they can be contacted in the future with the imagery only, others like the full ritual.

Finally, before I close this introduction, I want to share one last personal insight about these angels. Depending on where you are in your own personal evolution, where you are in time, what planets are transiting your houses, or who dominates- some of the angels are louder, or more easily heard than others. Although the lesser guardian angel is the Maître 'D of your experience, they are not always the one in the driving seat. Depending on what is happening, many factors will determine which of your angels are the ones in the driving seat.

I would like to conclude this introduction by wishing you fruitful experimentation with this book and a widening of both your perception and the dawning of you the magician, as co-architect of your existence.

David Cypher

Glastonbury

Lammas 2018

CHAPTER ONE

The Stage is Set

The Earth is our starting point; it is our home as we travel around the Sun, our star, each day. The Sun gives us life, as it does to all creatures and plants that share our home with us, and yet sadly, we, as a species, take it all for granted as we regularly abuse our fellow creatures and one another. Yet Earth is a remarkable place and one where we fulfil our individual destinies. Often in life, we wish for help, a little assistance perhaps, something which will give us an edge over our competitors or aid us as we struggle with our fate. Thus, there are times when those who know will approach the 'other realms' for help with their problems and vexations.

Whilst it appears that the sun is travelling around the earth, the reality is that the earth is moving around the sun. As the earth's poles are at an angle of 23 1/2° this allows the sun to appear as if it crosses the equator twice a year at both the spring and the autumn equinoxes, and as it does so, the day and night hours become of equal length. This is important because when the sun appears to travel north, as it does from the winter solstice to the summer solstice, as it crosses the equator, this heralds the sun's entry into the constellation of Aries, the start of the astrological year.

Visualised around the heavens is a great belt, the zodiac, against which the planets move, forming as they do various aspects from differing positions in the cosmos. Thus innumerable situations come into play in the lives of people, nations, and indeed all things and situations in life. As the earth rotates on its axis, the zodiac appears to move through the heavens and as it does so the positions of the signs move too. Therefore, during the twenty-four hours of the day, each sign will cross the ascendant, which is the point on the eastern horizon where the sky touches the earth. This is the point from which the twelve houses of the natal chart are calculated. As the zodiac is divided into 360° (a measurement from early Babylonia), it will take 4 minutes of time for a degree of the zodiac to cross the ascendant. For this reason, it takes two hours for each sign to cross over.

To each of these degrees of the zodiac is attributed an angel, and the angel who dwells at the degree from which one's natal houses originate will be the angel who wards that particular area of one's life. However, if you do not know your birth time and cannot, therefore, work out your natal chart with any degree of certainty, you may feel that this work has nothing to offer you. If you are in this position, do not despair, as you can still work with the angel who rules the degree where the Sun is domiciled on the day of your birth. An astrological ephemeris will show the degree of the zodiac that the Sun occupied on your day of birth, as it will all other planets too. The angel of the solar degree can be petitioned for help as an alternative to working with the natal angels generally.

The twelve houses of the natal chart are as follows, each house governing a particular area of one's life.

- **1st house:**
  This house is about you. It describes the individual, their attitude, behaviour and character
- **2nd house:**
  The individual's money and moveable goods, their possessions
- **3rd house:**
  Short journeys one may take, siblings, commerce
- **4th house:**
  The home, father, the end of life
- **5th house:**
  Sex, children, creativity, luck
- **6th house:**
  Health, employees, small animals
- **7th house:**
  Partners, spouses, friends, known enemies
- **8th house:**
  Other peoples' money, taxes, death
- **9th house:**
  Long journeys, banks, clergy, education, teachers
- **10th house:**
  The mother, career, how others see you
- **11th house:**
  Hopes and wishes, groups and organisations
- **12th house:**
  Self un-doing, hospitals, places of confinement, large animals, unknown enemies

Whilst this list is not exhaustive, and some authorities would dispute some of the areas given, they are however the areas considered vital by such astrological luminaries as the 17th-century astrologer William Lilly; whose work has much to commend it to the astrological student. Therefore, armed with one's natal chart (birth chart), which is a snapshot in time of the moment you were born, and considering in which degree each of the twelve houses falls in the chart, one can see which of the 360 angels will govern that particular area of one's life. From this, we can see which angel to work with to rectify any imbalance or disharmony in a specific area of life.

This can be approached through working with the angelic seals via candle magic, evocation or meditation, to name but three means to gain ingress to the angel's potentials. The present work will consider all these methods. Each angelic degree has a descriptive sentence which can be explored during meditation. The imagery built up via visualisation and the placing of one's consciousness therein will significantly activate the potentials of the degree in question, as you endeavour to work with the angel of that particular degree of the zodiac.

Kabbalistic thought will place the zodiac in Chockmah, the second sepheria on the Tree of Life; thus the twelve permutations of the Divine Name YHVH, being the God Name of Chockmah, will become the God Names of the twelve zodiac signs, and these will become the names that govern the energies of each sign.

- YHVH....Aries (YOD-HEH-VAV-HEH)
- YHHV....Taurus (YOD-HEH-HEH-VAV)
- YVHH....Gemini (YOD-VAV-HEH-HEH)
- HVHY....Cancer (HEH-VAV-HEH-YOD)
- HVYH....Leo (HEH-VAV-YOD-HEH)
- HHVY....Virgo (HEH-HEH-VAV-YOD)
- VHYH.....Libra (VAV-HEH-YOD-HEH)
- VHHY.....Scorpio (VAV-HEH-HEH-YOD)
- VYHH.....Sagittarius (VAV-YOD-HEH-HEH)
- HYHV.....Capricorn (HEH-YOD-HEH-VAV)
- HYVH......Aquarius (HEH-YOD-VAV-HEH)
- HHVY.....Pisces (HEH-HEH-VAV-YOD

CHAPTER TWO

The Twelve Tribes of the Zodiac

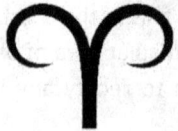

Aries

God Name....YHVH
Archangel....Malkidiel
Angel...... Sharhiel
Planet....Mars
Colour....Red
Incense.... Dragon's Blood

Invocation of Aries

Tu es ille Aries caeli claustra

Refringere iubet et nos in viam

Nostrum vitam activam

Cor nostrum impleatur animo

Preservere invictam ut vitae viam nostrum

Meaning:

Thou who art the ram of Heaven

break down the barriers upon our path

and lead us into active life

Let our hearts be filled with courage

so that we may persist unflinching upon our life's path.

Of the Angels of Aries and Their Seals:

1°.... Biael: Meditation Image: A man ploughing a large field.

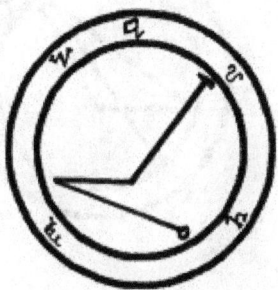

2°.... Gesiel: A man sitting at a table on which are scattered books and papers.

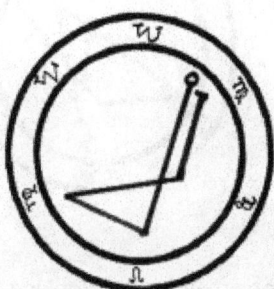

3°...Hael: A man on horseback wielding a sword as he approaches a company of armed men.

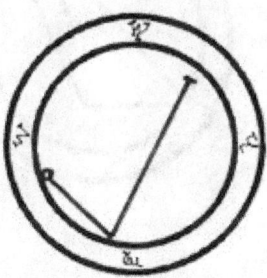

4°...... Vaniel: A man standing in a garden on a sunny day who is finely arrayed.

5°.... Zaciel: A large iron cross lying on the ground.

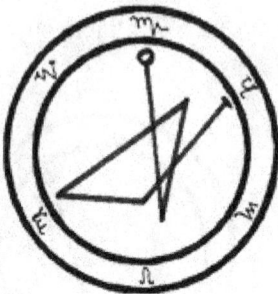

6° .... Cegnel: A horseman on a hill looking down at the people in the valley below.

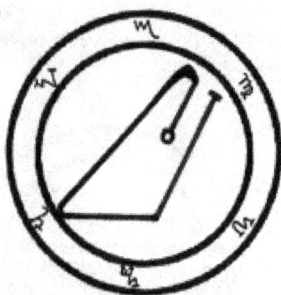

7°..... Japhael: A fox running beneath the shadow of a wall.

8°.... Itael: A man surrounded by others who are arguing with him.

9°.... Catiel: A man standing upon a high point and who stands with his arms folded.

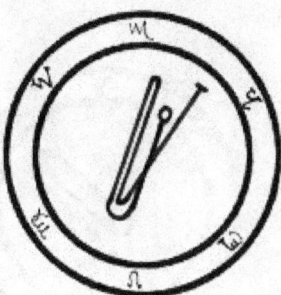

10°... Lariel: A lone horseman upon a battle field, surrounded by the dead and the dying.

11°.... Nathiel: A beautiful and kindly woman, standing robed and by herself, her left shoulder is uncovered.

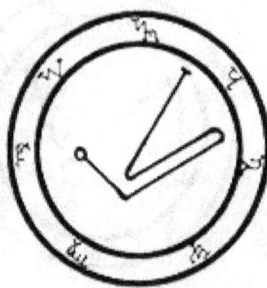

12°..... Sagnel: A man holding hands with two children.

13°.... Gabiel: A man standing upon a high mountain and is illumined by the setting sun. In his right hand he holds a staff and his left hand bears a crown.

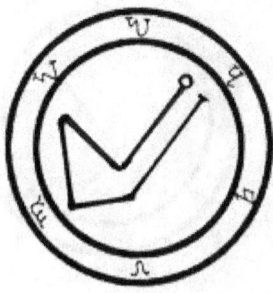

14°.... Pegiel: A distressed man adrift on a raft upon the ocean.

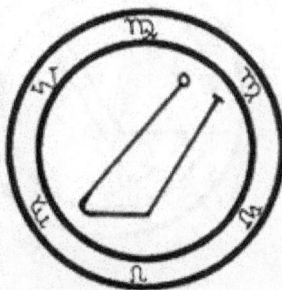

15°... Gadiel: A man struggling in the water with a broken footbridge above his head.

16°... Kheel: A young man who carries a book as he wanders through the trees, the sunlight shines through the branches upon him.

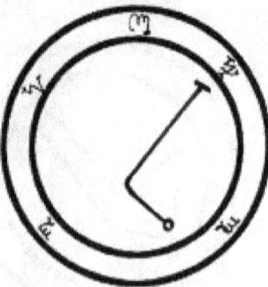

17°... Leviel: A woman who holds before her a set of scales. Upon one pan is a chalice of red wine; in the other is a pile of gold coins.

18°... Hezael: A man and a woman standing together and holding hands and smiling affectionately.

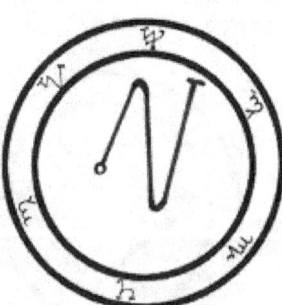

19°... Geciel: An old man dressed in a worn gown clutching two bags of coin to his chest.

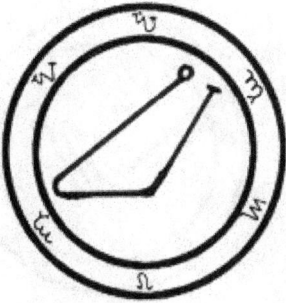

20°... Betiel: An armed man equipped for a long journey.

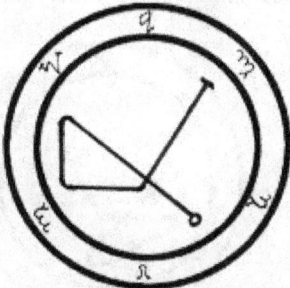

21°... Giel: A strong and prosperous man holding forth a chalice of wine.

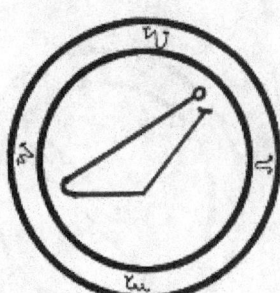

22°... Dachael: A man who is carrying water but stumbles and spills some upon the ground.

23°.... Habiel: *A man who stands with two others, holding a tankard in his hand, whilst his companions avert their gaze as they talk together.*

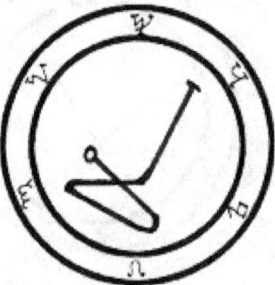

24°... Vagel: A man juggling with coloured balls; a naked woman stands behind him.

25°… Zadiel: A powerful man mounted upon a stallion.

26°… Cachel: A king who presents his sceptre to a kneeling man.

27°…. Tavael: A richly attired man who falls to the ground.

28°... Jezel: A lone woman who is beautifully clothed.

29°... Cechiel: A man felling a tree with an axe.

30°... Hetiel: A mounted knight looking at the waning moon.

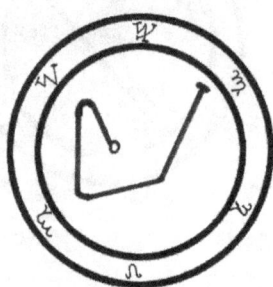

Taurus

God Name... YHHV
Archangel... Asmodel
Angel... Araziel
Planet... Venus
Colour... Red/orange
Incense... Storax

Invocation of Taurus...

Terra vitulum odites vir fortis et patiens

Da patientiam nostris conatibus nostris tua

Virtute et robore in omni opera

Meaning...

O thou mighty Bull of Earth

Thou who art patient and strong

Grant unto us endurance in our endeavours

Let thy power become our strength in all our undertakings.

Of the Angels of Taurus...

1°... Latiel: A black diamond-shaped figure.

2°... Hujael: A dying man lying upon the ground.

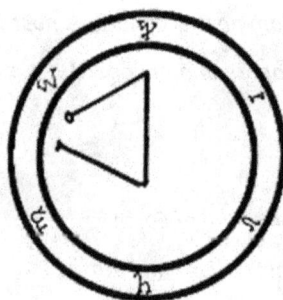

3°... Sachael: A woman picking grapes and filling her basket.

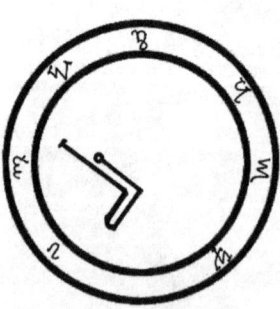

4°... Gneliel: A burning branch in the paw of a lion.

5°... Panael: A man cutting wood outside his cottage with sheep grazing in his orchard.

6°... Jezisiel: A middle-aged man standing upon a dais, he holds a scroll in his right hand and a laurel wreath is upon his head.

7°... Kingael: A cow grazing under a tree.

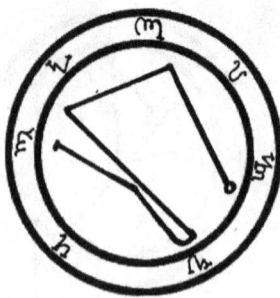

8°... Raphiel: A man dressed in rags who is gathering wood from the banks of a river.

9°... Tezael: A fat man walking among a flock of pigeons.

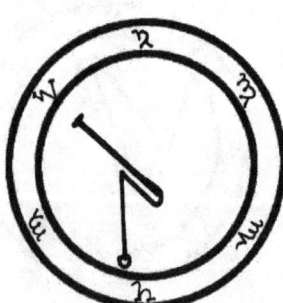

10°... Gnakiel: An ox who is asleep in a field, with two birds perched upon his back.

11°... Beriel: A kingly man seated upon his throne and bearing a sceptre, around him are bags of money.

12°... Gethiel: A bright orange flower upon which rests two butterflies.

13°... Dagnel: A dog running with a bone in its mouth, a second dog is chasing it.

14°... Vabiel: A bench upon which lies a wood plane and a right angle.

15°... Zegiel: A venerable man who is seated in a subdued light, before him are set several books.

16°... Chadiel: Two white cows are grazing on the edge of a jungle with a crouching tiger who unknown to them is about to spring.

17°... Tahiel: A man swimming against the current in a river and getting nowhere.

18°... Javiel: Two bulls fighting.

19°... Chazael: A woman lightly clad and lying in a field surrounded by violet-coloured flowers.

20°... Bachiel: A crow standing upon a pot.

21°... Getiel: An owl who is perched in a tree, in the tree branches a snake is coiled.

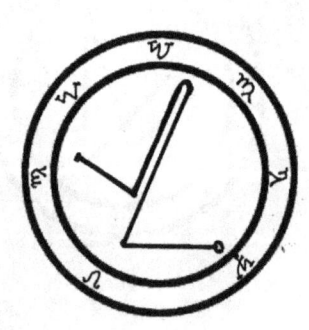

22°... Dajiel: A tree standing in a meadow with bees working the blossom.

23°... Hachael: A king sits upon his throne, behind him stands a figure veiled in black.

24°... Vabiel: A bed of a dried-up river, crows are feeding therein.

25°... Zagiel: A lion rampant, standing upon elevated ground.

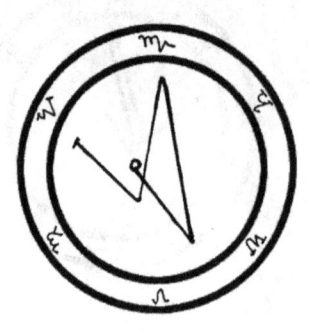

26°... Chadiel: A fair woman leading a child by the hand and gathering flowers.

27°... Gehiel: An alchemist at work in his laboratory, upon his bench is much gold.

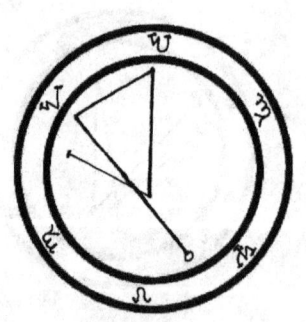

28°... Javael: A man climbing a pole set on a hill.

29°... Chasiel: A powerful man driving two manacled slaves with a scourge.

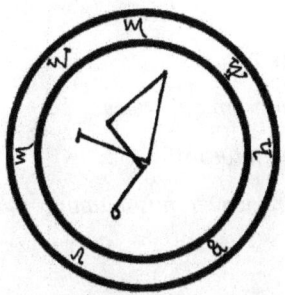

30°... Sachael: A dark man in costly garments, surrounded by his servants as he reclines upon a couch.

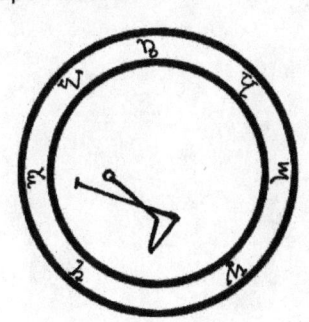

♊

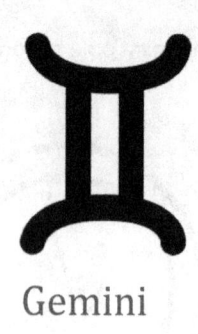

Gemini

God Name... YVHH... (YOD-VAV-HEH-HEH)
Archangel...Ambriel
Angel...Sarayel
Planet...Mercury
Colour... Orange
Incense...Wormwood

Invocation of Gemini...

Signo geminorum quia tu es

Sanctus Dei naturam

Separatio invocaverimus te unum

Meaning...

O thou Holy Twins for thou art the sign of divine duality.

The separation in unity...for thee we invoke.

Angels of Gemini

1°... Latiel: Two yellow flowers growing under a tree.

2°... Nagael: A man climbing over a wall with a rope ladder.

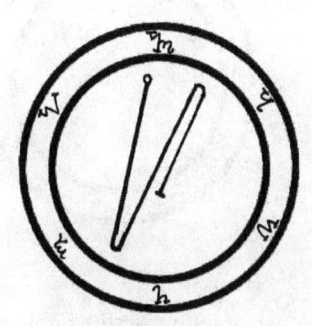

3°... Sachiel: A troubadour who stands next to a waterfall listening to the sound of the falling water.

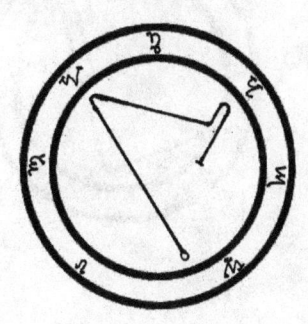

4°... Gnaliel: A man dressed as a minister of state and who is both kindly and wise.

5°... Paniel: Two men standing in a wood and preparing to fight a duel. Between them is a box of jewels.

6°... Tzaniel: A woman standing with a book in one hand and a pair of scales in the other.

7°... Kingael: A peaceful valley with high mountains in the distance. In the valley is a lake upon which a swan is floating.

8°... Raphiel: A burning house in the night.

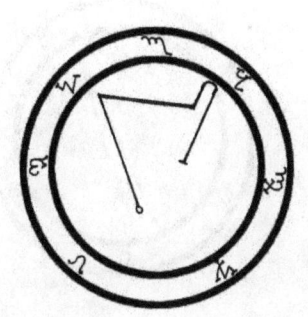

9°... Gnetiel: The figure of a woman holding a globe in one hand and a sceptre in the other.

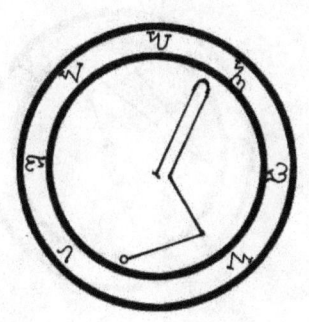

10°... Bakiel: A pretty woman handing a child a glass of water.

11°... Geriel: Gypsies sitting around a cauldron in which food is cooking.

12°... Dathiel: A laurel tree broken in the wind.

13°... Hegnel: Two wolves who are feeding in the moonlight.

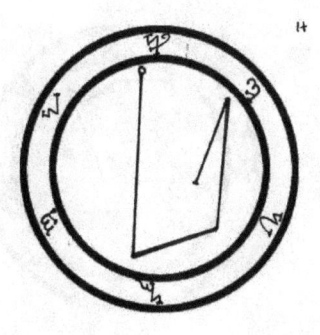

14°... Vabiel: A masked man standing beneath a tree at night.

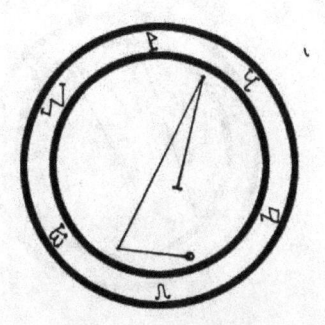

15°... Zagiel: A woman holding a bundle of sticks, her hair is loose and blowing in the breeze.

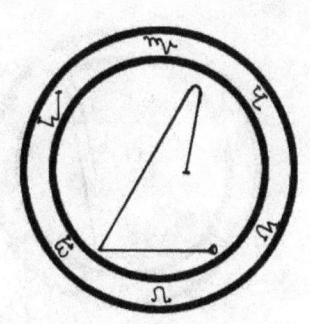

16°... Chadiel: A man squatting and breaking stones with a hammer.

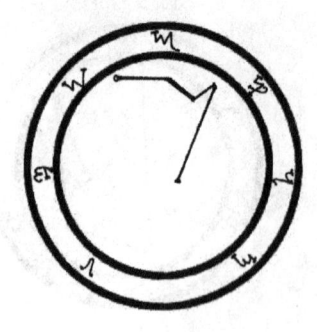

17°... Tahiel: A broken jug lies upon the ground around which lie fruits.

18°... Javiel: An arrow in motion.

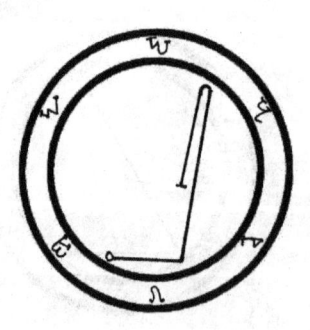

19°... Chazael: A naked woman stands dejected; her hair hangs over her breasts.

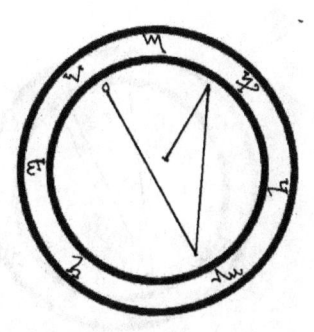

20°... Bachiel: Two men stand together, one holds the bridle of a horse.

21°... Getiel: A youth is seen throwing coins in the air and catching them in a cup.

22°... Dajiel: A woman who is lying under a tree and feeding the birds.

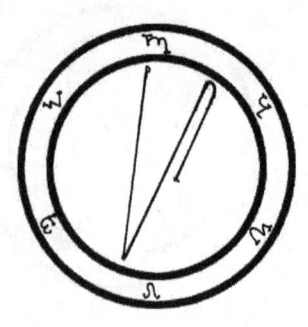

23°... Hachael: A bare oak tree which has been struck by storms and stands upon a bleak moorland.

24°... Vabiel: Several sparrows are dust-bathing together.

25°... Zagiel: A old book lying upon a table and beside it is a burning lamp.

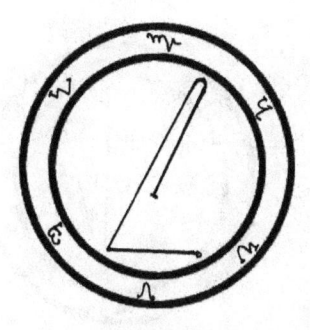

26°... Chadiel: Several men arguing in the market square.

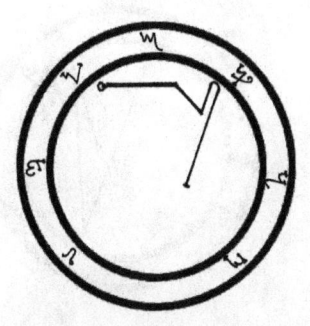

27°... Tahiel: A dishevelled young man who sits upon a bare rock by the sea and weeps.

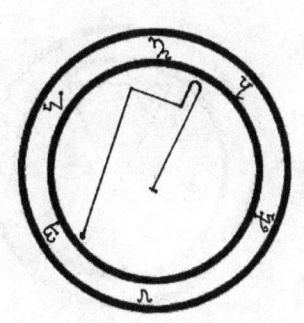

28°... Daviel: A fertile field.

29°... Heziel: A gloomy sky with strong winds blowing clouds and flocks of birds hither and thither.

30°... Vachael: A wolf stalking a lone sheep.

Cancer

God Name....HVHY (HEH-VAV-HEH-YOD)
Archangel... Muriel
Angel... Pakiel
Planet... Luna
Colour... silver /white
Incense... Jasmine

Invocation of Cancer...

Quia tu, Domini es, qui est creatura Cancer maria

aeternitatis qui docet ad nos in periculo caute et tenacityatem Teneamus armisque quae ad illud quod est creatura societatem donare digneris cum teritur nostris

Meaning...

For thou O crab who art the creature of the oceans of eternity who shows unto us caution and tenacity in the face of danger. Let us hold on to that which is worthy and discard that which is worn. In our companionship with creation

Angels of Cancer...

1°... Sachiel: A vine, heavy with fruit hangs upon an old wall in the sunshine.

2°... Metiel: A dog standing over a bone with two other dogs watching.

3°... Asel: A seated woman who is crying, her hair and clothes are disheveled, she holds a bunch of fading lilies and roses.

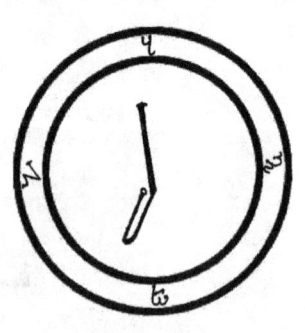

4°... Sachiel: A table upon which are the remains of a meal.

5°... Mihel: A young tree bent and twisted.

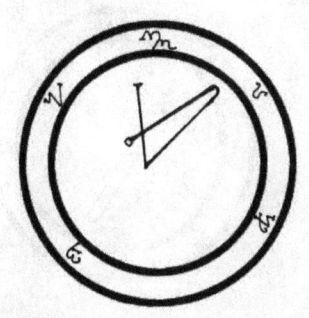

6°... Aniel: A gaudily dressed woman who holds jewellery in her hand.

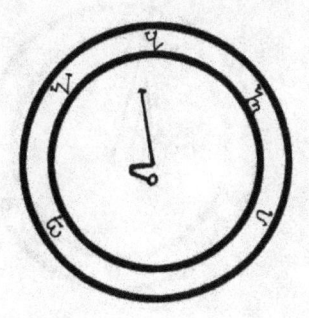

Liber Angelorum

7°... Sasael: A gauntlet, sword and a scourge lying upon a tree stump.

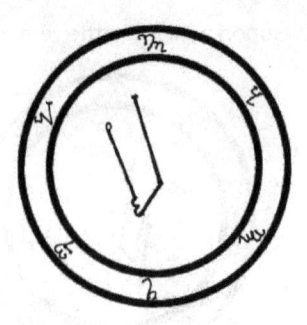

8°... Magnael: A dove lying upon the ground with a serpent poised to strike.

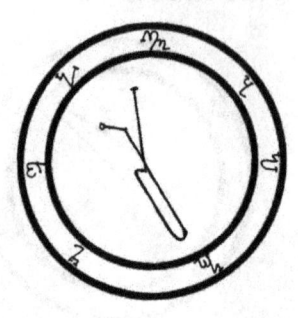

9°... Aphiel: A village within a fertile valley.

10°... Sersael: A wide spread oak tree around the roots of which are many young shoots. Birds sing in the branches.

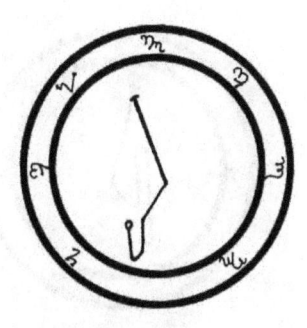

11°... Makael: A stranded boat upon a beach.

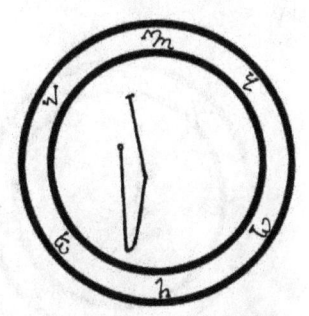

12°... Ariel: A dagger beside a skull.

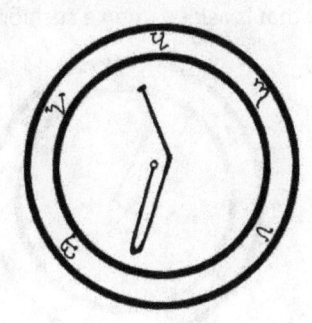

13°... Sethiel: A caduceus between two moons, one crescent the other gibbous.

14°... Magnael: A bunch of flowers over which shines a bright star that sparkles in the night sky.

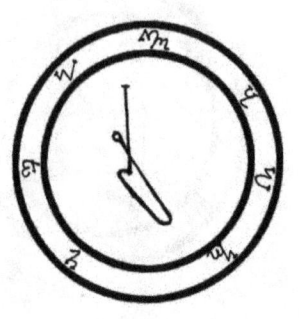

15°... Abiel: A dog that is asleep upon a cushion which is on a throne.

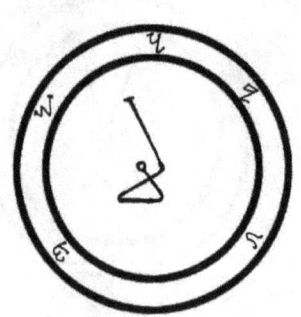

16°... Sagel: Samson standing over a dead lion.

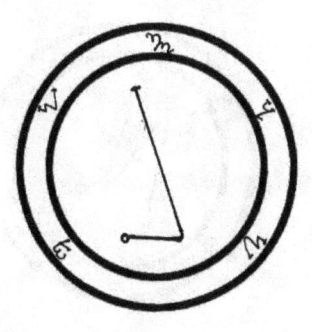

17°... Madiel: A flash of lightning.

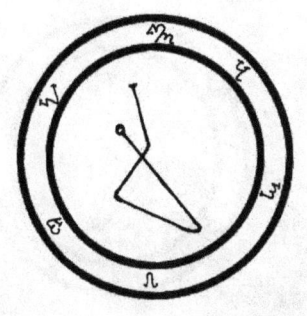

18°... Athiel: A bunch of faded flowers, sickly and sweet-smelling.

19°... Savael: A harp.

20°... Maziel: A man riding a frisky horse.

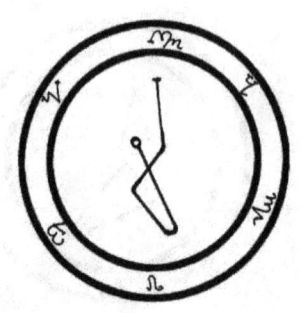

21°... Achiel: A becalmed ship at sea, a waning moon dimly lights the scene

22°... Setiel: A man sleeping upon the ground with tools beside him.

23°... Maiel: A man stands upon a mountain top with a staff in his hand. The sun is setting behind him.

24°... Achael: A strong castle upon a rock, upon the battlements flies a flag with a crown upon it.

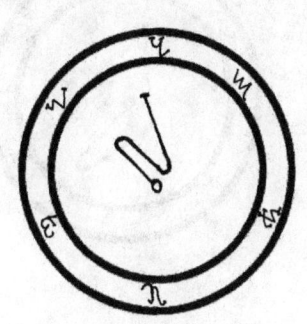

25°... Sabiel: Armed horseman riding towards a wood.

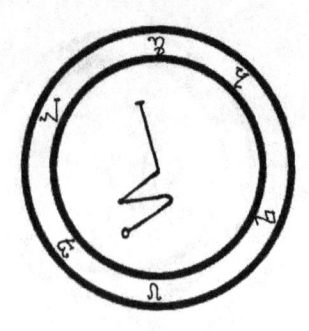

26°... Magiel: A falling star.

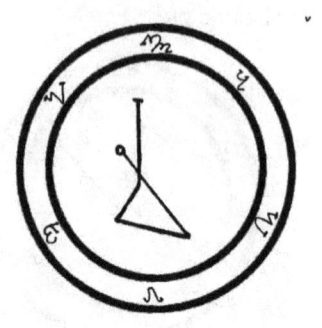

27°... Adiel: A young ox harnessed to the plough.

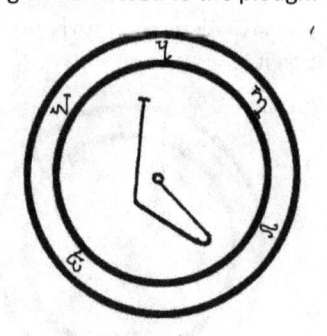

28°... Sahiel: A beautiful rural view.

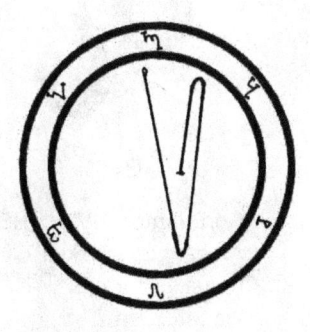

29°... Meviel: A tiger stalking a horse.

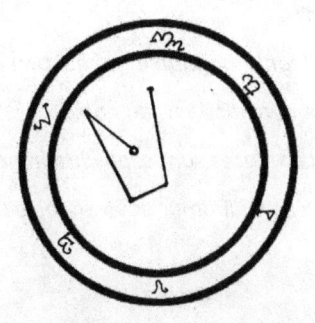

30°... Aziel: *A young horse running across a field.*

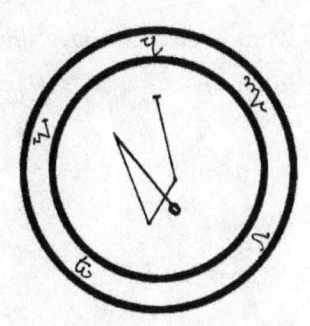

♌

Leo

God Name... HVYH (HEH-VAV-YOD-HEH)
Archangel... Verkiel
Angel... Sharatiel
Planet... Sun
Colour... Gold
Incense... Frankincense/Cinnamon

Invocation of Leo...

Tu facies leonis magnanimum qui omnes sine timore virtute

et actione benedictionis da nobis.

Ferum lucere faces sunt sepulchra in novissimis tuis

et praesta ut inlueamur adversa facie terroris.

Meaning...

O thou Lionhearted one who faces all life fearlessly

Grant unto us the blessing of action and courage.

Fierce are the fires that shine in the depths of thine eyes.

Grant that we may look upon adversity and tremble

not before its terror.

Angels of Leo...

1°... Mechiel: A lion standing upon a high point looking towards the rising Sun.

2°... Satiel: A windsock fluttering.

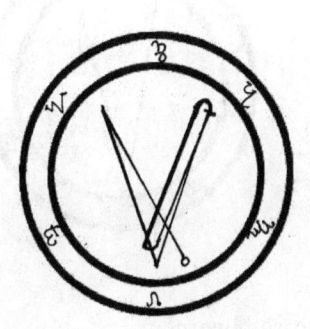

3°... Ajel: A beam of light shining through the mist.

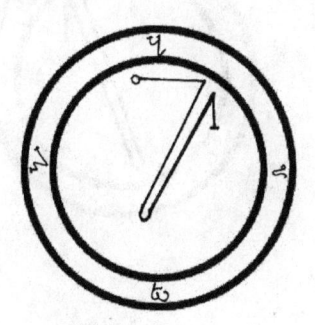

4°... Mechiel: An alert cat watching for movement.

5°... Sahel: A snake coiled around a tree and ready to strike.

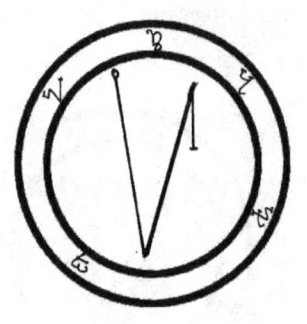

6°... Aniel: Two crossed swords.

7°... Masiel: A diamond set upon a sceptre that catches the light and shines brightly.

8°... Sengael: A triangle of fire set in the clouds, in which shines a bright eye.

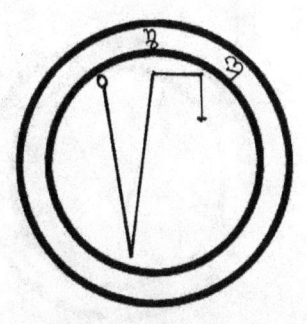

9°... Aphiel: A large house set in a beautiful garden in which struts a peacock.

10°... Metziel: A broken oak tree underneath which is a skeleton.

11°... Sekiel: A man and woman are seated at a table upon which is a jug of wine.

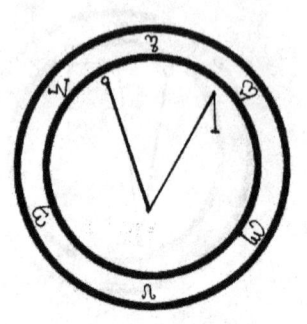

12°... Ariel: A white bull is grazing in the shade of a large tree.

13°... Gnethiel: A jutting rock upon which grows a clump of grass.

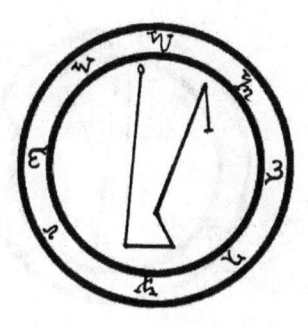

14°... Sagiel: A broken wheel lying upon the ground with a horse grazing nearby.

15°... Abiel: A figure like the angel of the Sun standing erect and striking the earth with the point of a dazzling sword.

16°... Magiel: A ram stands upon a barren rock.

17°... Sadiel: A man riding a camel with attendants following.

18°... Athiel: A bright mirror in which reflects the Sun.

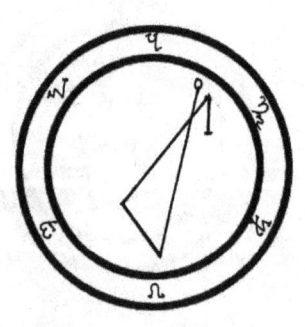

19°... Muviel: A man dressed in rags and running into a strong wind and getting nowhere.

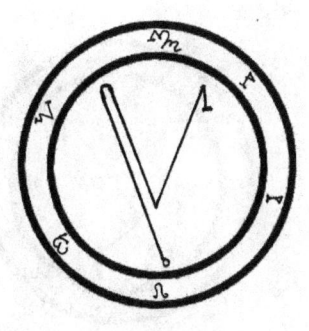

20°... Saviel: A crescent moon joined to a shining star.

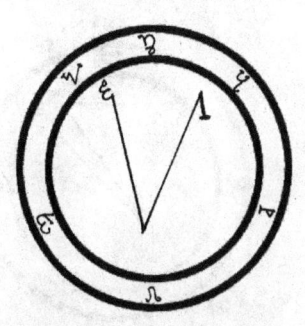

21°... Achiel: A human face surmounted by a coiled serpent; they raise a hand.

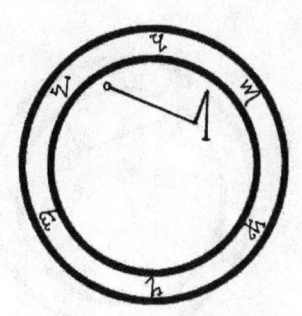

22°... Metiel: A hawk hovering over a nest of young birds.

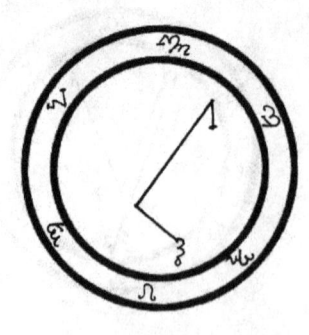

23°... Siel: A bright pale star shining over a clear lake.

24°... Achael: A woodcutter felling a large tree.

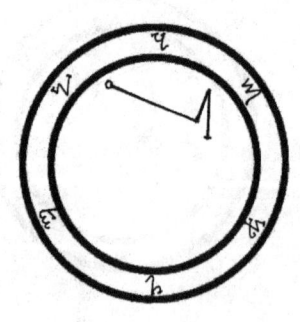

25°... Mabiel: A triangle with its apex pointing at the ground.

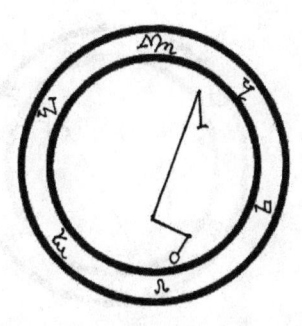

26°... Sagiel: A man ploughs a field with oxen; a wood stands to the side of the field.

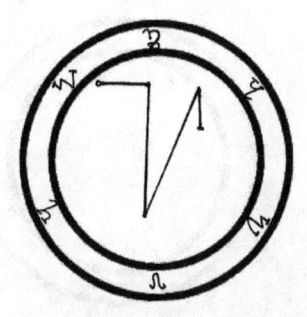

27°... Adiel: A dagger.

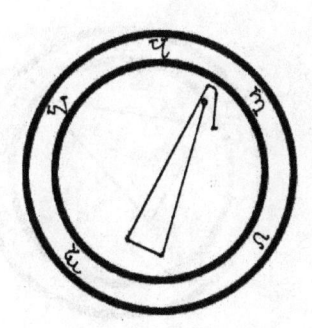

28°... Mahiel: Two hands linked in friendship.

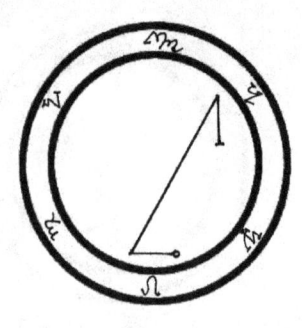

29°... Savael: Two golden circles joined by a blue ribbon which is tied in a double bow.

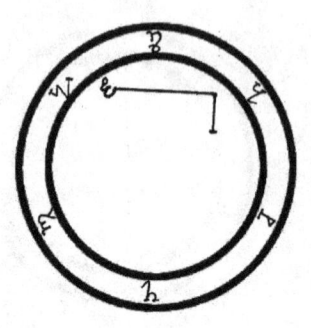

30°... Aziel: A starving dog cringing and whining.

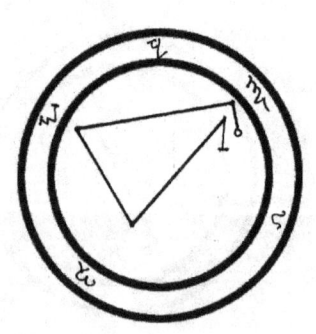

♍

Virgo

God Name... HHVY (HEH-HEH-VAV-YOD)
Archangel... Hamaliel
Angel... Shelathiel
Planet... Mercury
Colour... Golds and Russets of Autumn
Incense... Mastic /Mace

Invocation of Virgo...

O tua virgo in mundum retinere tuam priman

puritatem manuum hominum esset in terra

quae nobis sorte vera laetemus in es

quod nobis et sacro velamina mysteriorum salua.

Meaning...

O thou Virgin of the world retain thy primal purity.

O Earth by the hands of man be thou our true inheritance.

Let us rejoice in that which comes to us untarnished

so that the holy veil before the mysteries remains inviolate.

Angels of Virgo....

1°... Celiel: People gathering for a village festival.

2°... Senael: A solitary rock in a desert.

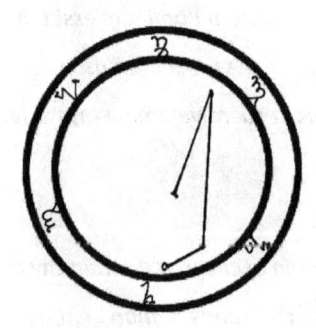

3°... Nasael: A man wearing a skull cap and busy with his books.

4°... Sangiel: A ripe field of corn.

5°... Gnaphiel: A soldier armed and ready for war.

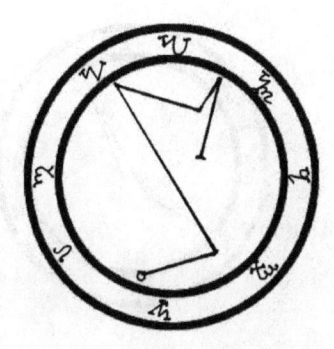

6°... Paziel: A man and woman sitting at a table with a jug of wine and some flowers.

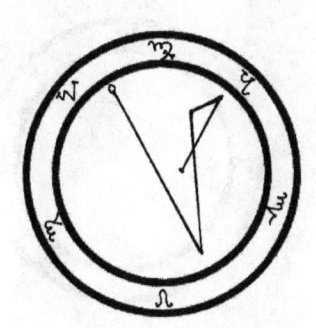

7°... Tzakiel: A man and woman standing, their backs to one another.

8°... Kriel: A tower stands on a hill which is surrounded by a wood.

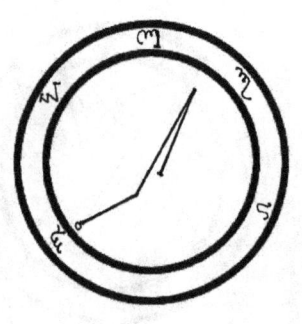

9°... Rathiel: A stagnant pool filled with weeds.

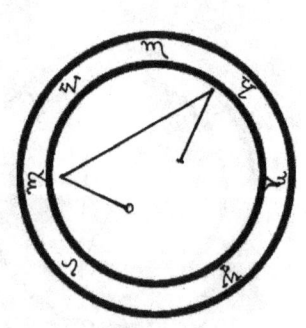

10°... Tangiel: A masked woman at a table on which is a money bag.

11°... Gnasiel: A hand with the index finger pointing upwards.

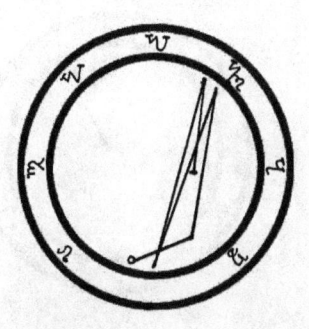

12°... Bagiel: A man leading a blindfolded woman.

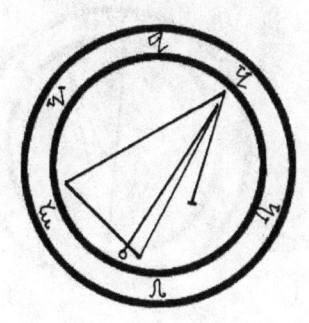

13°... Gediel: A river flowing through open fields, the moonlight glints upon the waters.

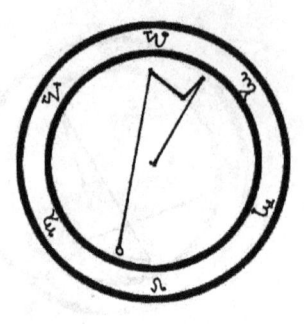

14°... Dahiel: A miner digging into rocks.

15°... Hevael: A beautiful woman holding a dove in each hand.

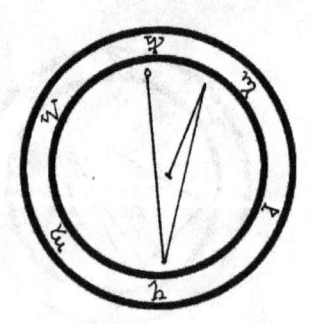

16°... Vaziel: Several men standing together and talking.

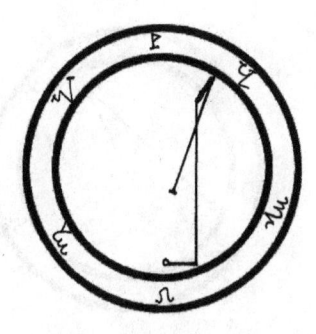

17°... Zachiel: A old man harvesting grapes.

18°... Chetiel: Happy children surrounding an old white-headed man.

19°...Tiiel: A farmer with a whip in his hand.

20°... Jechiel: A man dressed in black watching two swordsmen.

21°...Cabiel: A man carrying a money bag in each hand.

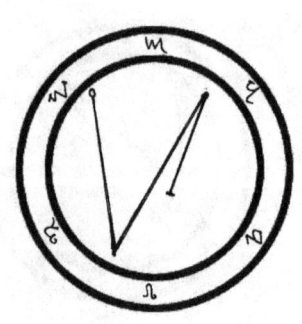

22°... Bagiel: A evil woman standing before a mirror.

23°... Gediel: A ship in full sail.

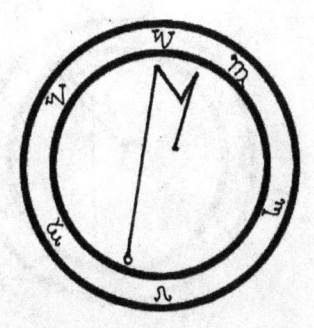

24°... Dahiel: A naked man sitting on a rock by the sea, he covers his eyes with his hands.

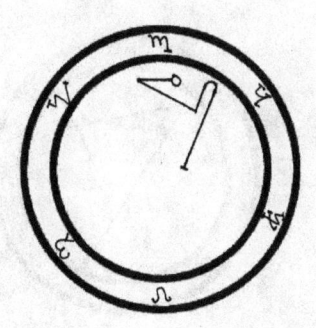

25°... Hoviel: Crossed swords over which is a crown.

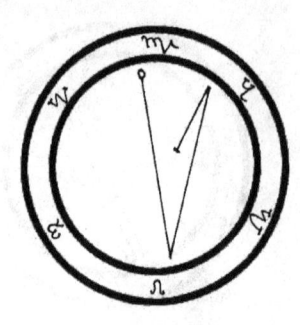

26°... Vaziel: Two women who are arm in arm and talking together.

27°... Zachiel: A broken hammer lying upon a work bench.

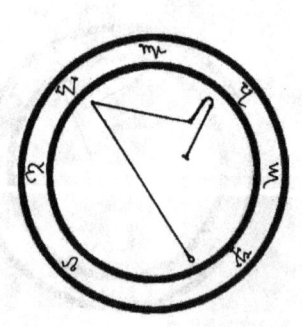

28°... Chetivel: A tree laden with fruit.

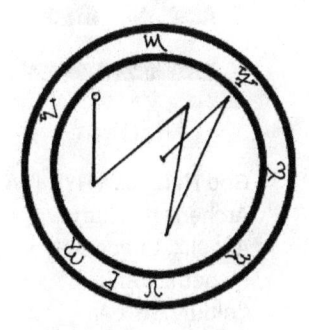

29°... Tajael: A cardinal.

30°... Jachiel: A headless man standing.

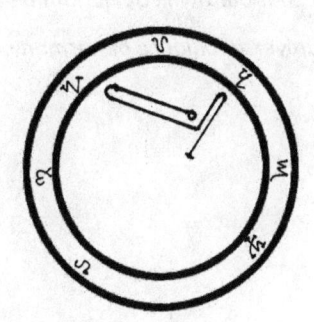

Libra

God Name.... VHYH (VAV-HEH-YOD-HEH)
Archangel.... Zuriel
Angel.... Chedeqiel
Planet.... Venus
Colour.... Green
Incense.... Galbanum

Invocation of Libra

Qui enim statera iusta intra beatitudinis nostrae

non habens libram stateram in commoveri

non deesse nobis triue proenire aequilibrium reconcilietur

Concordia universalis statera.

Meaning...

For thou who art the balance that holdeth our happiness

within thy scales let not our balance be disturbed.

Let us not be lacking in our own balance

and grant that our own equilibrium be at one

with the universal balance of harmony.

Angels of Libra....

1°... Ibajah: A man with a sword in his hand.

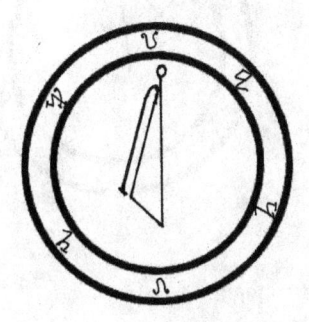

2°... Chaiel: A monk who is a healer.

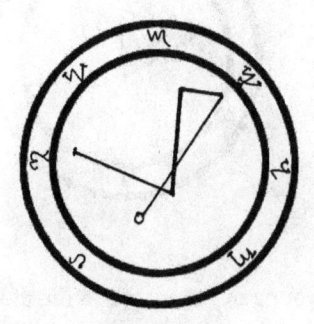

3°... Sahael: A man who is chained.

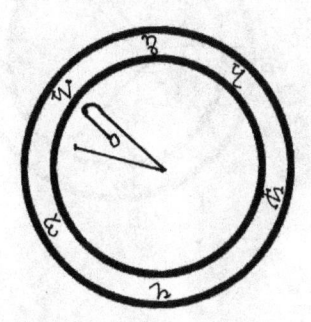

4°... Naviel: A ploughman with a broken plough.

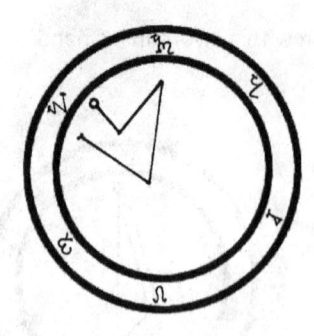

5°... Saziel: A red triangle.

6°... Gnachiel: A young ox harnessed to the plough.

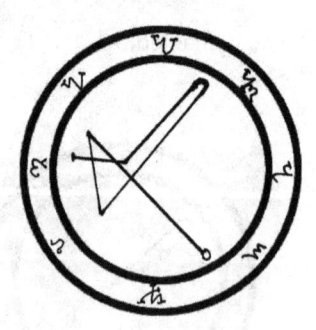

7°... Patiel: A naked man falling from a high point into a deep lake.

8°... Trajael: A young girl weeping over a grave.

9°... Kachiel: A gladiator who is armed and ready to fight.

10°... Baliel: A prison door fitted with iron spikes.

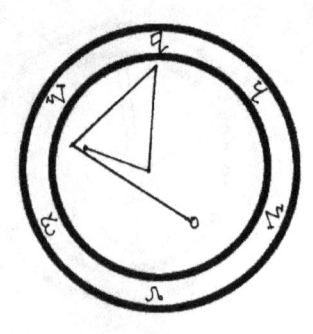

11°... Tamael: A centaur armed with a bow and arrow.

12°... Gnamiel: A woman looking at her reflection in a hand glass.

13°... Bangiel: A pillar of black marble standing upon a rock.

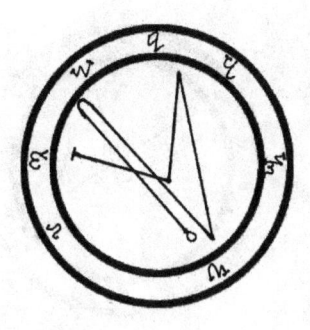

14°... Gepheel: A mask.

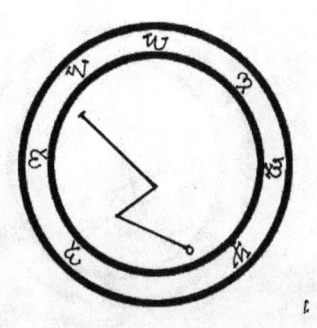

15°.... Datziel: A man walking with two women, one on each arm.

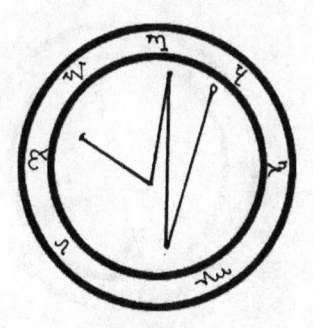

16°... Hekiel: An ice-burg framed by the aurora borealis.

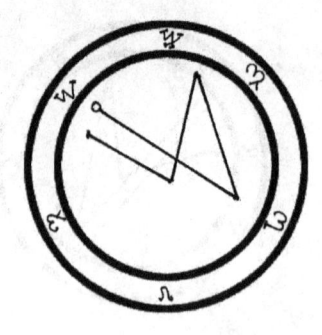

17°... Variel: A dagger stuck in an old door.

18°... Zethiel: A house with an open door.

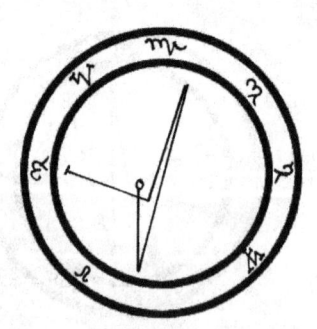

19°... Chengiel: A square of black marble upon which is inscribed a sceptre and a crown.

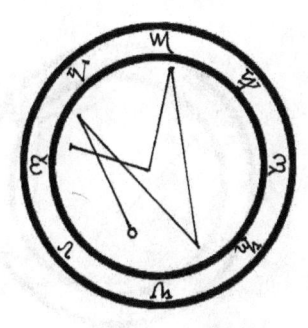

20°... Tibiel: A priest standing in the light from a window.

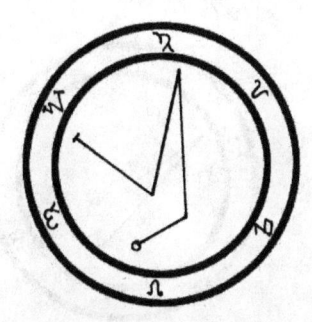

21°... Jagiel: A dilapidated bridge spanning a dry river bed.

22°... Cediel: A man asleep by his money bags.

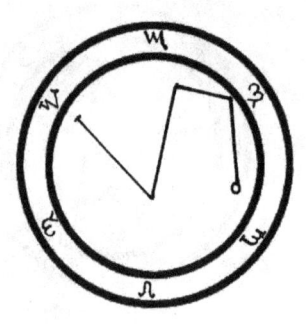

23°... Behel: An old man wearing a gown and a skullcap.

24°... Gevael: A solitary tree standing upon a rocky height behind which is a dark cloud.

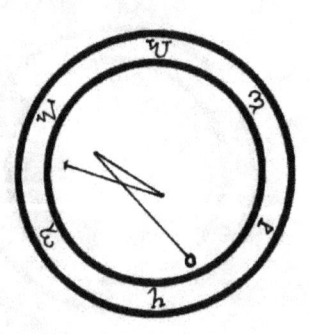

25°... Daziel: An elevated promontory illuminated by the noonday sun and crowned with many flowers.

26°... Heckiel: A knight ready to attack.

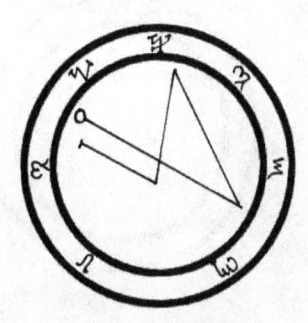

27°... Vatiel: A spreading cedar tree under which is a cottage.

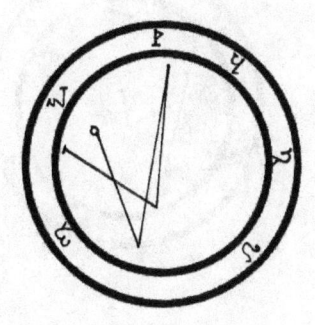

28°... Zajel: A donkey tethered to a grinding wheel.

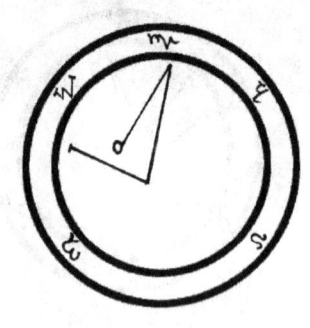

29°... Chechiel: A dark pool surrounded by vegetation.

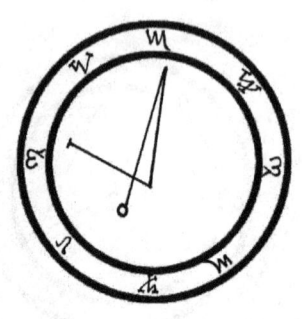

30°... Tehiel: A man asleep, over him hovers a vulture, a serpent is ready to strike him and a leopard about to attack.

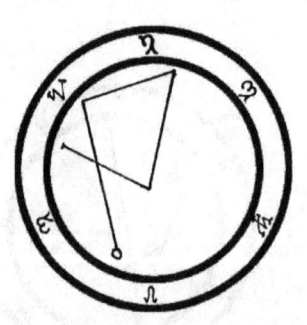

♏

Scorpio

God Name... VHHY (VAV-HEH-HEH-YOD)
Archangel... Barkiel
Angel... Saitzel
Planet... Mars
Colour... Red
Incense... Oppopanax

Invocation of Scorpio...

Aquila propter quod verum serpentum

da nobis aquam ut magis conquisitio

animas reficiantur in arcano sanctorum

scientia et sapientia

Meaning...

For thine is the eagle and the serpent

Grant unto us the true water of the wise

so that our souls may be refreshed

in our holy quest for the hidden knowledge

and the eternal wisdom.

Angels of Scorpio...

1°... Teliel: A nomad armed with a spear.

2°... Jeniel: The sun rising over a sea cliff.

3°... Cesiel: An old man sitting under a tree, his head is bowed.

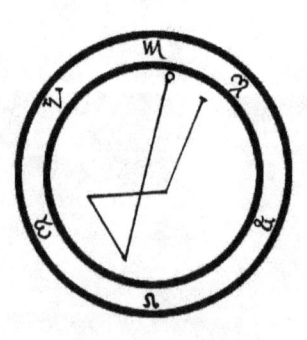

4°... Lengael: A lyre upon which is hung a laurel wreath.

5°... Naphael: A storm-swept prairie.

6°... Satziel: A flowering shrub growing upon a mound of soil.

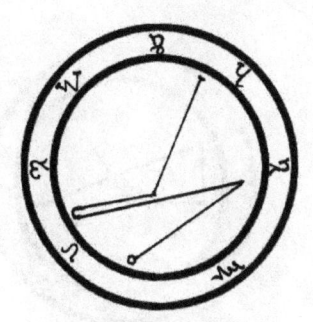

7°... Gnakiel: A man standing with a spade resting on his shoulder and a pick-axe at his feet. He holds a bright jewel which is reflecting in the sunlight.

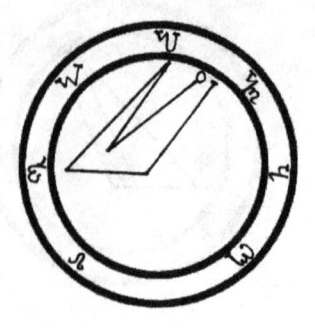

8°... Periel: An archer shooting at a flock of birds.

9°... Tzethiel: A bird's nest on the ground in which are the young.

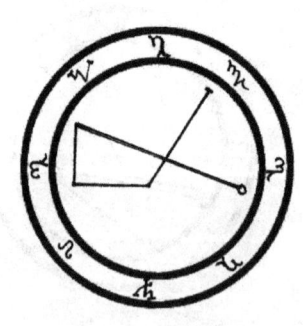

10°... Rengliel: A masked man.

11°... Rebiel: A hare seated upon a knoll, the moon shining behind it.

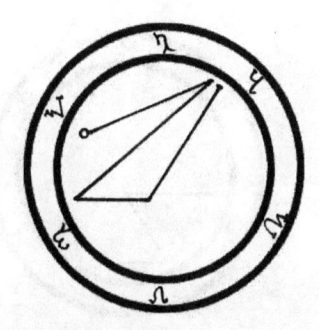

12°... Tagiel: A cottage in a wood.

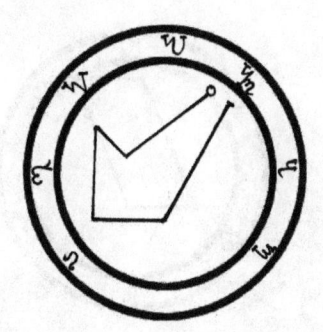

13°... Gnadiel: A strong tower upon a rock.

14°... Bevael: Two men seated at a table and drinking wine.

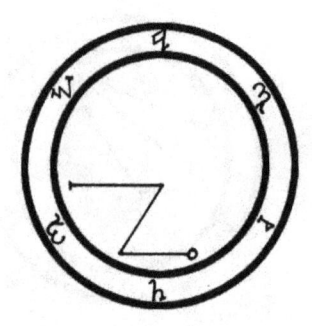

15°... Geziel: A bear asleep under a tree in which is a swarm of bees.

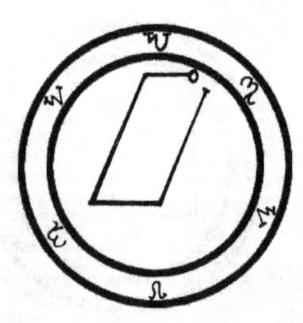

16°... Dachiel: A chalice from which a red light shines forth.

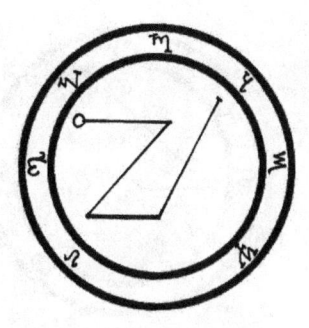

17°... Hephiel: A battered ship lying upon the sea shore.

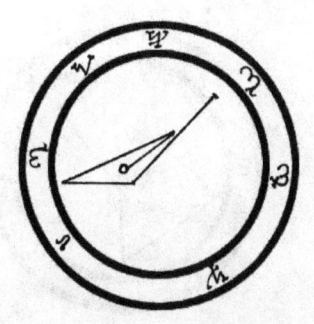

18°... Vagael: A woman who is charming snakes, one is about her neck.

19°... Zackiel: A sharp knife.

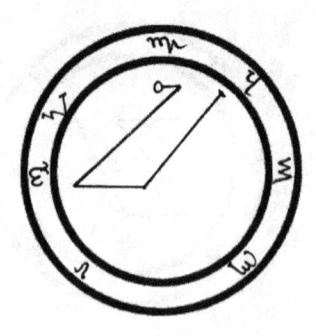

20°... Chabiel: The Sun rising over the sea.

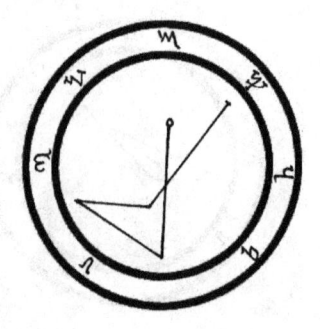

21°... Tagiel: A bull pawing at the ground and snorting.

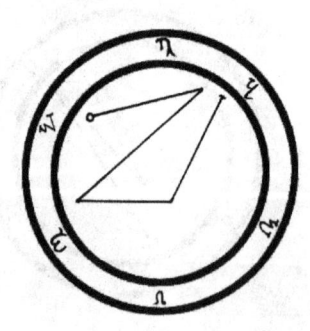

22°... Jadiel: A waterfall falling over.

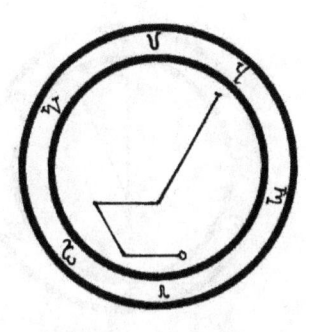

23°... Cahael: A man sowing seeds in the wind.

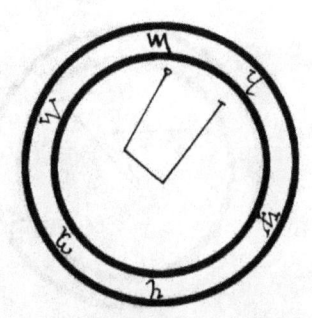

24°... Baviel: A woodcutter hewing timber next to a wooden hut.

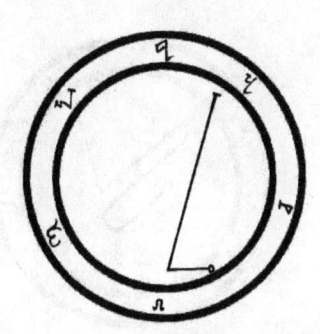

25°... Gezael: A wolf standing upon the carcass of a horse.

26°... Dachael: A swimmer in an angry sea.

27°... Hatiel: A warrior haranguing armed men.

28°... Vajael: A rock upon which is standing a stone cross which is haloed by the rising sun.

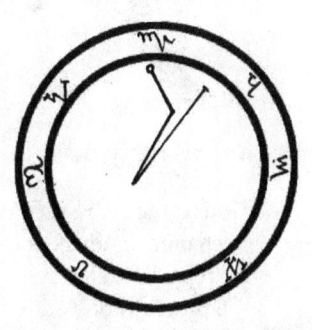

29°... Zachiel: A man seated at a table upon which are sheets of paper held down by pebbles.

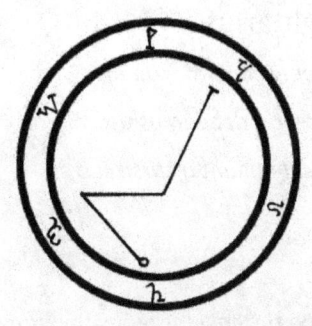

30°... Chasiel: A robed woman holding a wand around which is coiled a serpent.

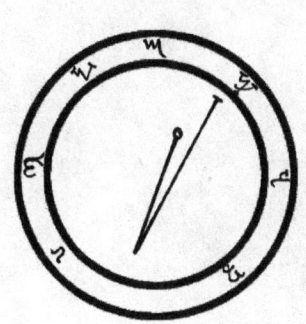

Sagittarius

God Name... VYHH (VAV-YOD-HEH-HEH)
Archangel... Advakiel
Angel... Saritiel
Planet...Jupiter
Colour...Blue
Incense... Cassia

Invocation of Sagittarius...

Sancti et very copiam scopum

Tua notare iter debeamus ascendere

et non declinabaunt a cursu suo

Meaning....

Let truth be thy holy target as thy arrows

mark our path that we follow

Let our aim be true that we not swerve from our final goal

Angels of Sagittarius

1°... Taliel: A man lying by the roadside.

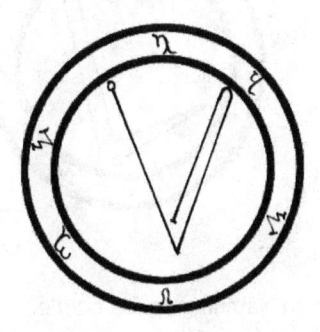

2°... Janiel: A man armed with a sword.

3°... Casiel: The Goddess of Mercy enthroned.

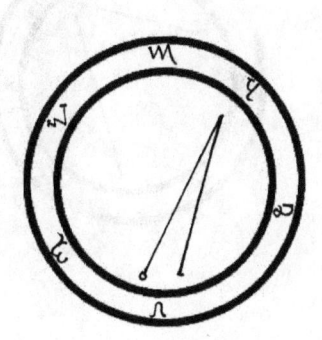

4°... Langael: A soldier armed with a crossbow.

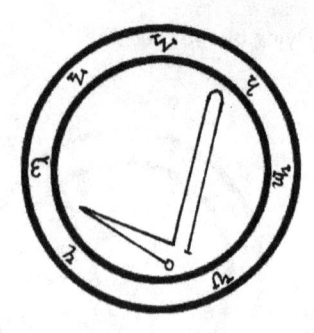

5°... Naphael: A man watching over a cradle.

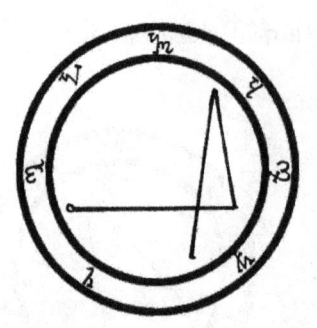

6°... Satziel: A windmill turning.

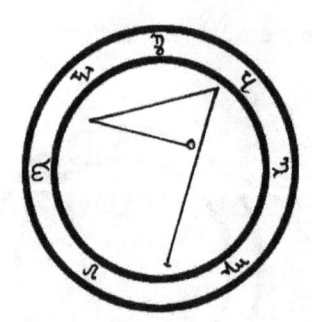

7°... Gnakiel: A herd of cattle grazing in the sunshine.

8°... Periel: Two men playing cards.

9°... Tzangiel: A house on fire.

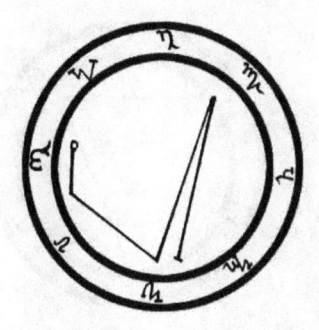

10°... Jebiel: A full moon shining in a clear sky.

11°... Regael: A crouching tiger.

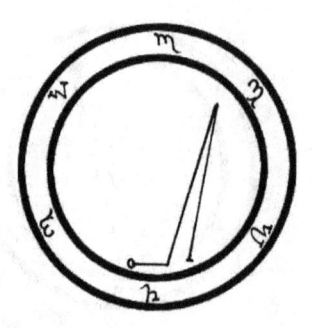

12°... Tediel: A woman disporting herself upon a couch.

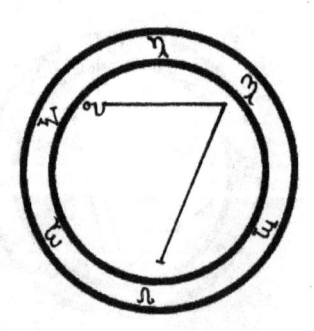

13°... Gnaheel: A portcullis.

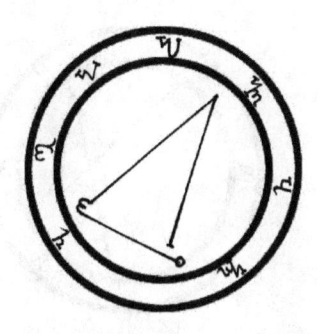

14°... Bevael: A disorderly pile of books.

15°... Geziel: An arrow in mid-air.

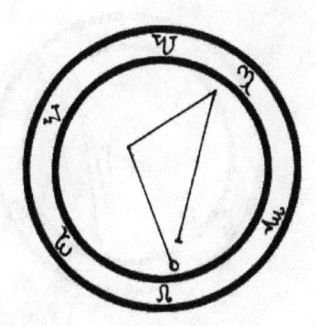

16°... Dachiel: A cave set in a cliff face.

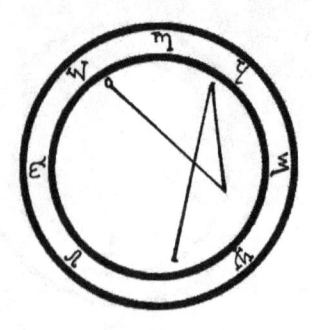

17°... Hephiel: A man on a raft.

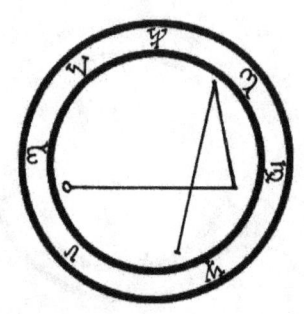

18°... Vagael: A man's face that is painted and surrounded by a tangle of hair.

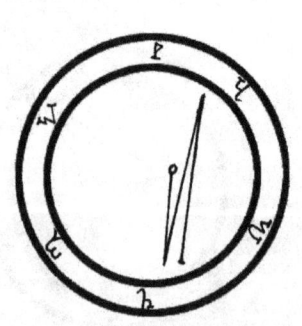

19°... Zackiel: A serpent that is surrounded by a ring of fire.

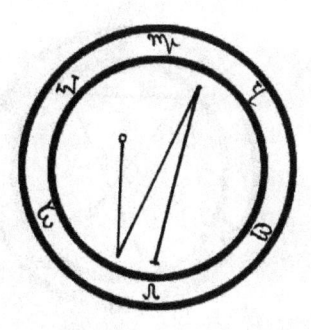

20°... Chabiel: A garden in flower.

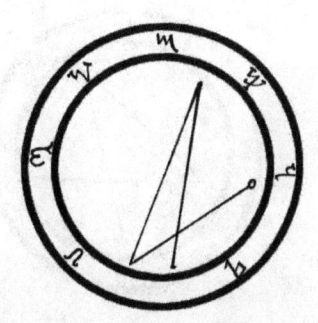

21°... Tagiel: Two interlaced triangles with a third superimposed.

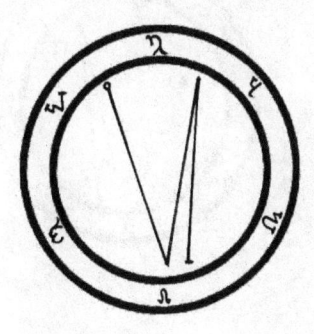

22°... Jadiel: Two arrows crossed.

23°... Cahael: A heart that is encircled with a band of iron and is pierced by a jeweled dagger.

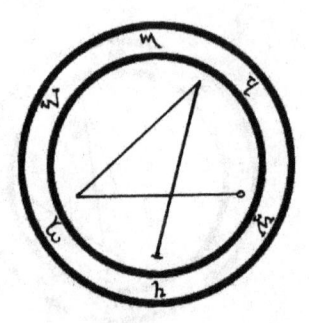

24°... Baviel: A broken tree that is struck by a lightning bolt.

25°... Gezael: Three goblets of wine upon a table which are placed as a triangle.

26°... Dachael: A mask shaped as a dog.

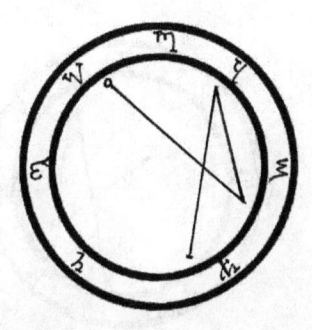

27°... Hatiel: A man lying beneath the paw of a lion.

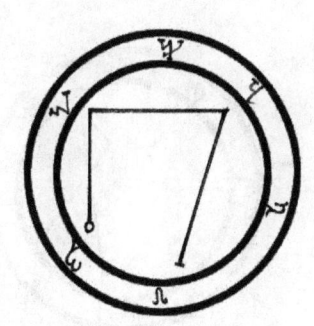

28°... Vajael: A tortoise.

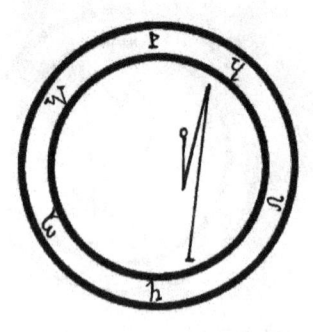

29°... Zachiel: A hare.

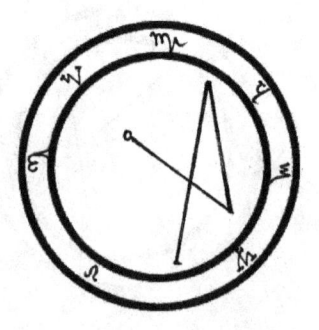

30°... Chasiel: A spade that is struck into the soil.

Capricorn

God Name... HYHV (HEH-YOD-HEH-VAV)
Archangel... Hanael
Angel... Sameqiel
Planet... Saturn
Colour... Black
Incense... Myrrh

Invocation of Capricorn....

Qui enim habet antiqua mysteria

hirclum luce media inter cornua caestus

super excels terra qui es virtus viget autem et concede

nobis famulis personam ut supera assequi monte sancto

Meaning...

For thou who art the Goat of the Ancient Mysteries

who holds upon high the light between thy horns.

Thou who art the power of earth personified

grant unto us thy vitality and vigour

so that we may gain the heights of the holy mountain

Angels of Capricorn

1° ... Chushel: A boy and girl standing with their arms entwined.

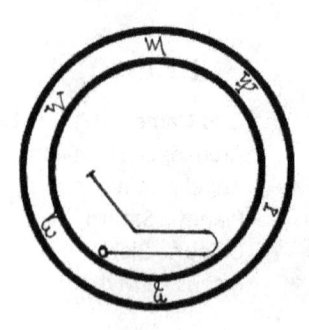

2° ... Temael: A weather vane pointing north.

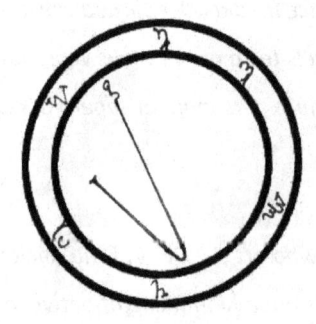

3° ... Jaajah: A serpent which is coiled around an uplifted torch

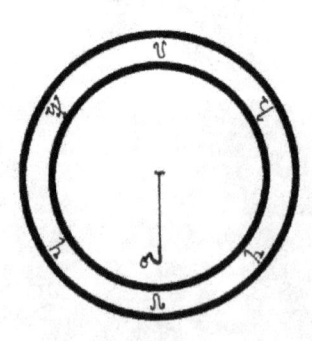

4° ... Cashiel: A lamp burning brightly.

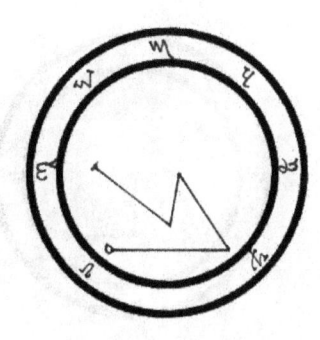

5° Lamajah: A cottage with the door standing wide open.

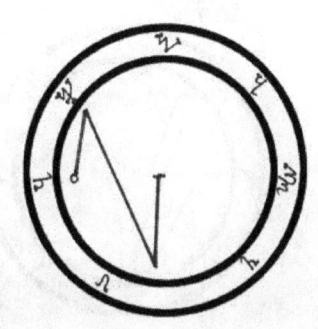

6° ... Naajah: A heart which is surrounded by a golden light.

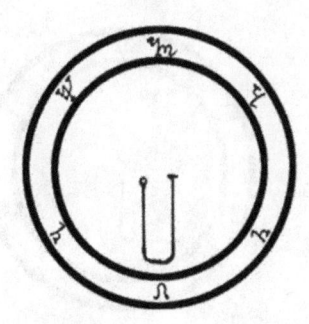

7° ... Sasajah: A heart pierced by nails.

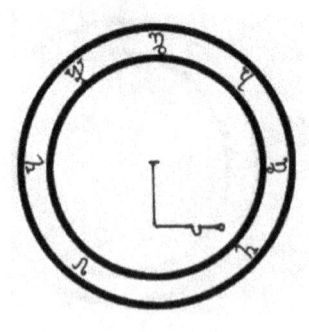

8° ... Gnamiel: An eagle flying high with its prey.

9° ... Paajah: A cross with a broken key upon the ground.

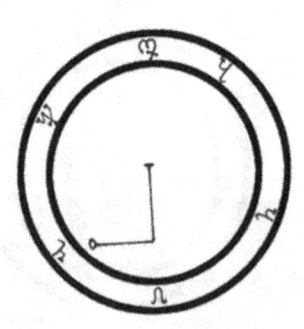

10 ... Izashiel: An owl sitting in the moonlight.

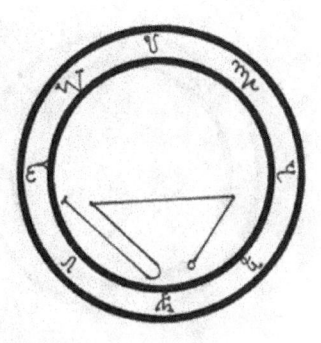

11 ... Kmiel: A roll of parchment sealed and placed across a scepter.

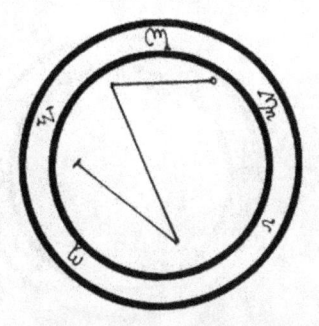

12 ... Riajah: A fox running in the moonlight.

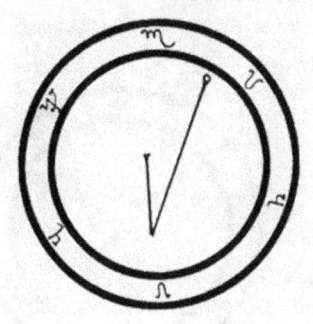

13 ... Tashiel: A tripod with flames leaping from the brazier.

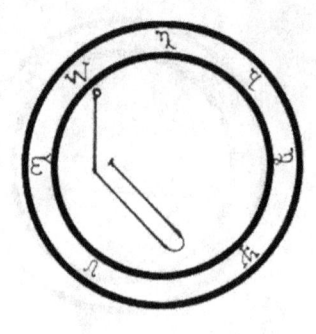

14 ... Gnamiel: A harrow standing in an open field.

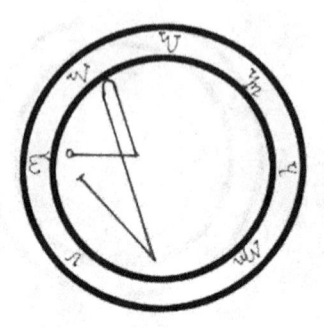

15 ... Baajah: Soft clouds upon the horizon.

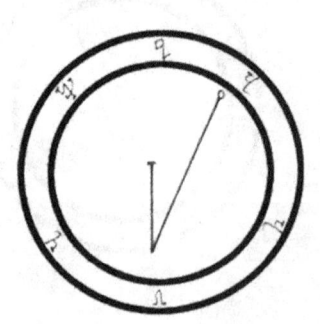

16 ... Gashiel: A man galloping upon a horse.

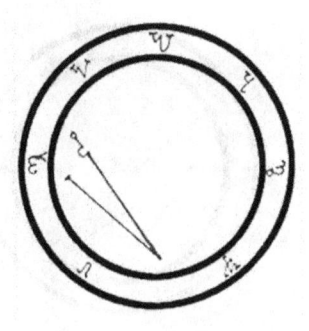

17 ... Dashiel: A harp lying upon a wreath of flowers.

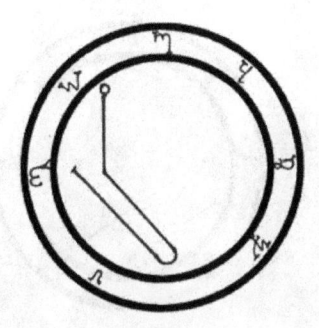

18 ... Haajah: Two men fighting together.

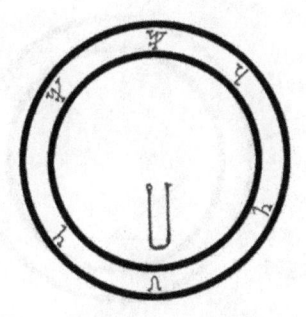

19 ... Vashiel: A rock protruding from a turbulent sea.

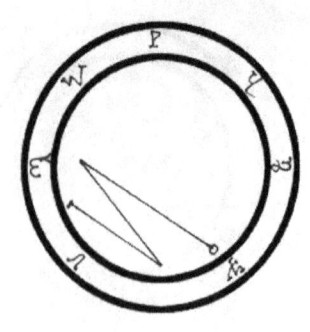

20 ... Zamiel: An ape seated before a mirror.

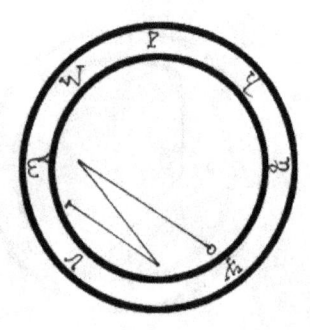

21 ... Chael: A manuscript upon which rests a retort and crucible.

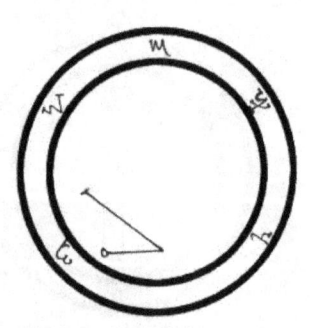

22 ... Tashiel: A plough.

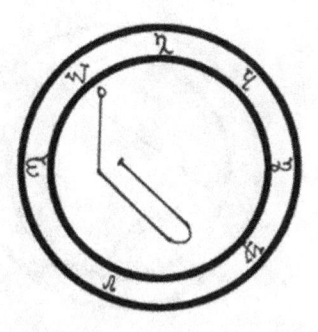

23 ... Jashiel: An overturned wine glass.

24 ... Ciajah: A tankard that is set upon a table.

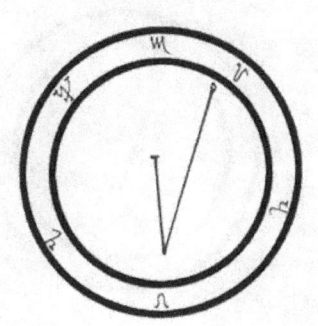

25 ... Beshael: Bubbles floating in the air.

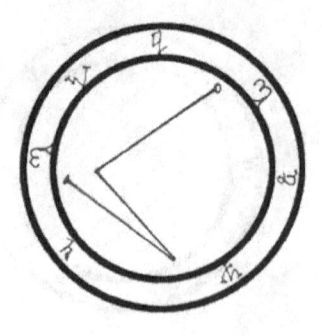

26 ... Gamael: Distant boats upon the sea.

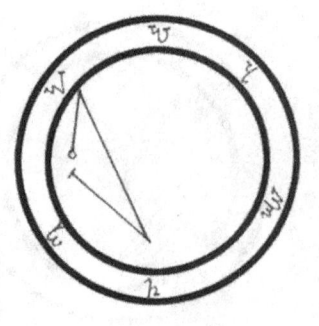

27 ... Daal: Fields fringed with woodland.

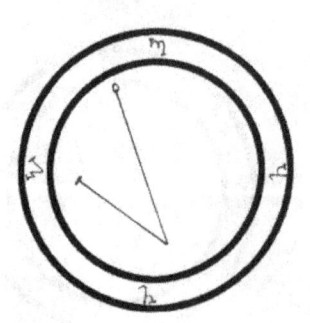

28 ... Heshael: A sextant and compass.

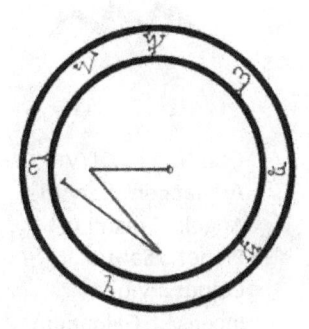

29 ... Vamiel: A dark pool over hung with trees.

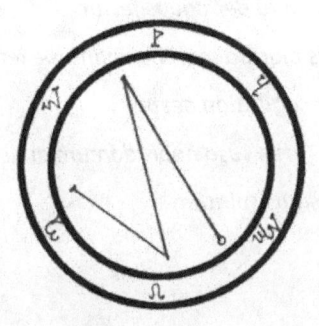

30 ... Zaajah: An arrow in flight.

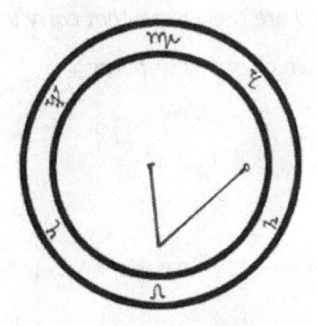

Aquarius

God Name... HYVH (HEH-YOD-VAV-HEH)
Archangel... Kambriel
Angel... Tzakmiqiel
Planet... Saturn
Colour... Violet
Incense... Galbanum

Invocation of Aquarius...

Aerea quem tu per aquas fertur

Possumus placido mari navigantes exerceant in nobis

sensus et cogitation aestus

Beati qui fertis vasa nobis domum quae

nos accipimus spiritum

Meaning....

O thou Airy One by whom is carried water

May we sail serenely upon the sea of consciousness

and let us travel freely on the tides of thought

For blessed are the vessels that carry us and we welcome

the wind which brings us home

Angels of Aquarius

1 ... Chamiel: A man sleeping upon sheaves of corn.

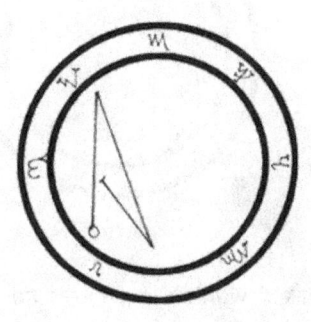

2 ... Tesael: A book on which is standing a compass and an hour glass.

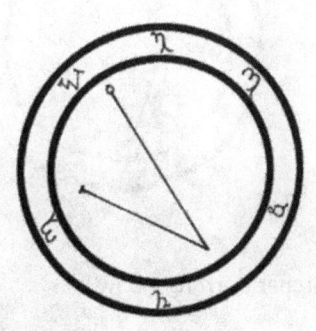

3 ... Jaaheh: A man walking with bended head and leaning upon a staff.

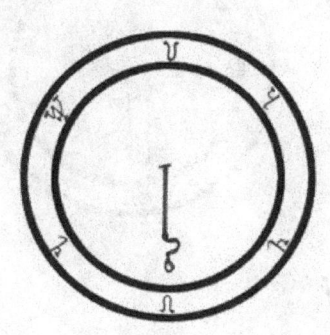

4 ... Camiel: A Chinese man dressed in a robe of purple and gold.

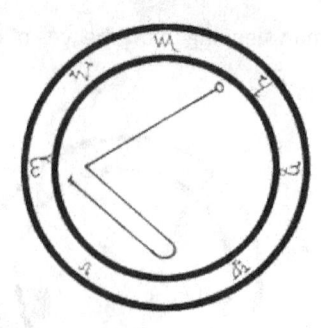

5 ... Lashiel: A naked woman looking at her reflection in a pool of water.

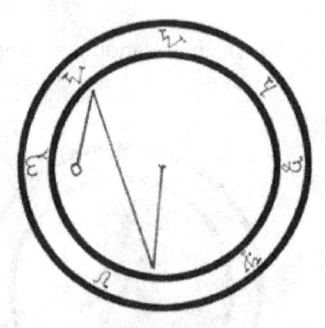

6 ... Naajah: An archer drawing a bow.

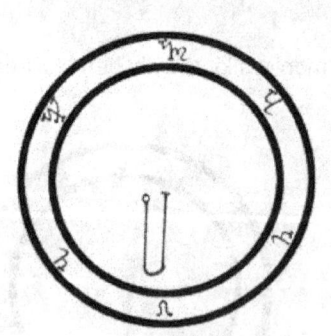

7 ... Samiel: A target that is stabbed with a sword.

8 ... Gnashiel: A lion standing in an open arena.

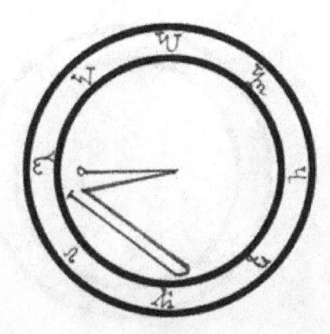

9 ... Paajah: A rock that has been split by a flash of lightening.

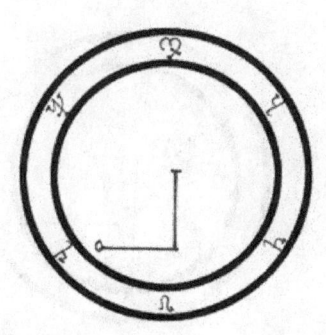

10 ... Izamiel: A head and hand lying separated from the body.

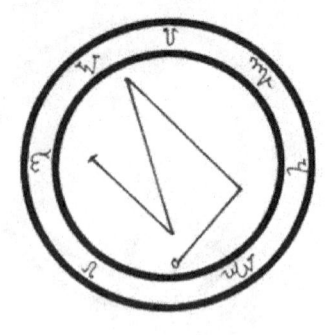

11 ... Kshiel: Two bulls fighting on a cliff's edge.

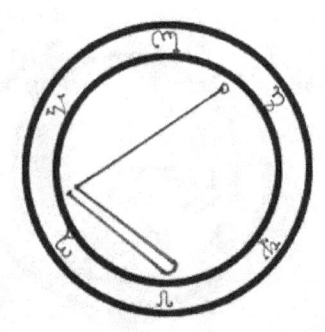

12 ... Raajah: A lion raging against the bars of its cage.

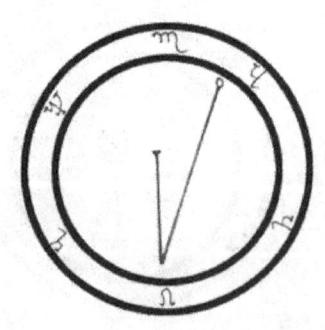

13 ... Tamiel: An armed cavalier.

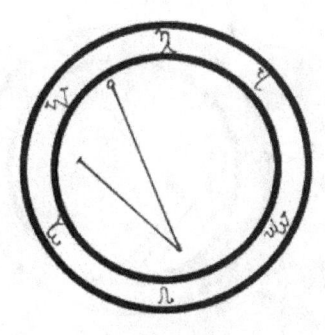

14 ... Gnashiel: A broken bridge over a fast-flowing stream.

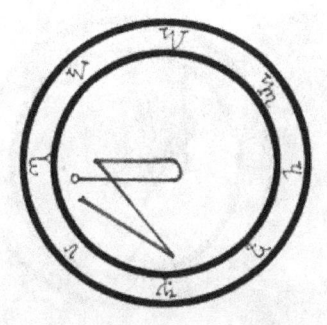

15 ... Baajah: A ship in full sail upon a sunlight sea.

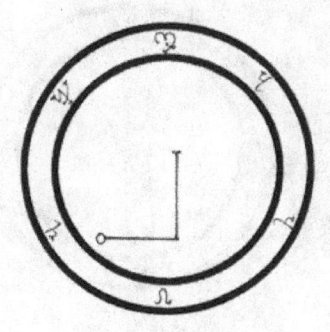

16 ... Gashiel: A smith's forge and bellows.

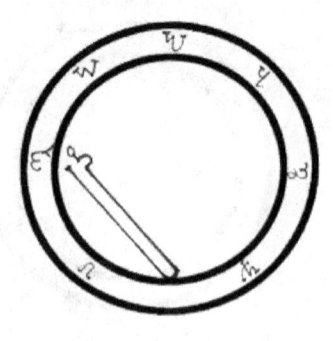

17 ... Dashiel: A sick man lying upon his bed.

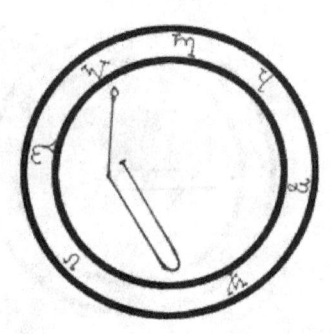

18 ... Haajah: An old woman wearing a hooded cloak sitting upon a stool.

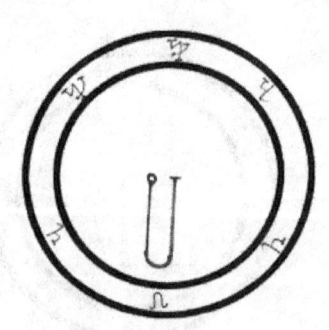

19 ... Vashiel: A boat upon the sea with a man clinging on to it.

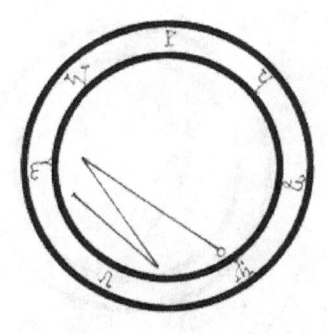

20 ... Zamiel: A tortoise.

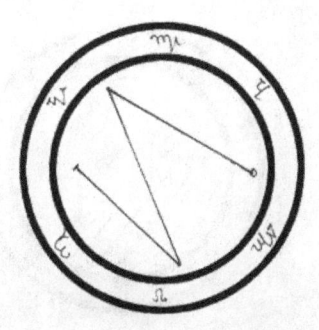

21 ... Chael: A wounded man lying on the ground.

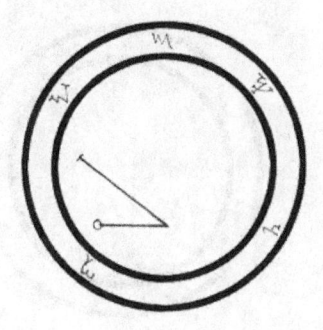

22 ... Tashiel: A raging bull fighting a dog.

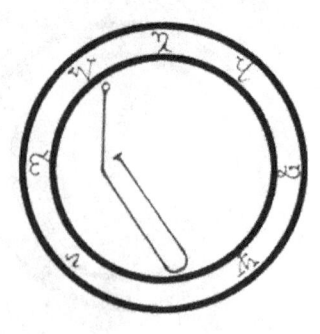

23 ... Jashiel: A beaver gnawing at a tree that overhangs a cliff.

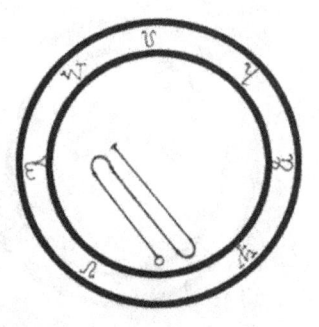

24 ... Ciajah: A stalk of wheat.

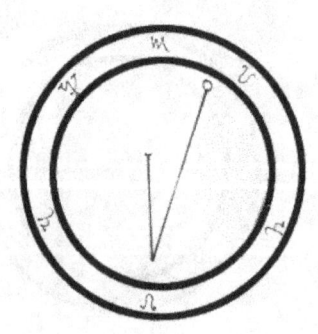

25 ... Beshael: A dark angry face with a red streak upon the brow.

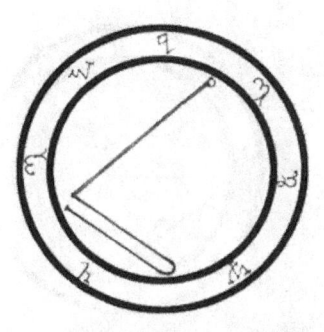

26 ... Gamael: A blindfolded man walking towards a pit.

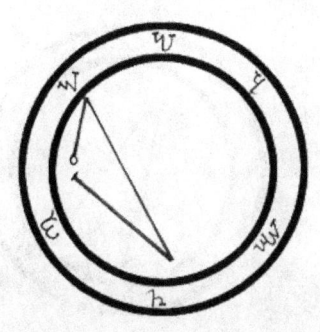

27 ... Daael: A stately mansion surrounded by trees and parkland.

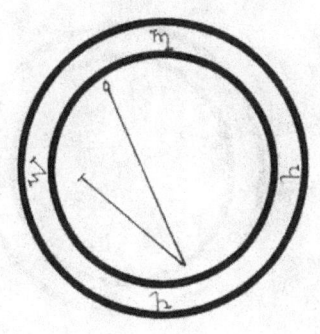

28 ... Heshael: A cup, a pack of cards and a dice.

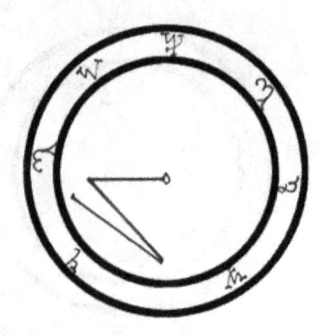

29 ... Vamiel: Two crossed swords surrounded by a laurel wreath.

30 ... Zaajah: A sceptre surrounded by a crown.

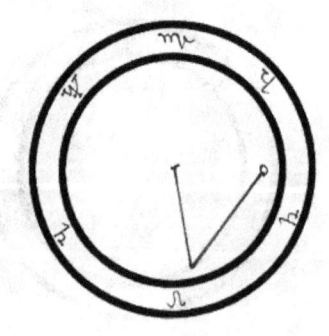

Pisces

God Name... HHVY (HEH-HEH-VAV-YOD)
Archangel... Amnitziel
Angel... Vakabiel
Planet... Jupiter
Colour... Crimson
Incense... Ambergris

Invocation of Pisces....

Tu piscis fines orbis creation et nos in profudum

maris emergere de quibus ad finem nostri itinerio merguntur

Sed ne pereamus beate vivere

rursus aquam regenerationis

Meaning...

For thou art the fish that finalize the cycle of creation

we emerge out of the depths of the ocean and into them

we are plunged at the end of our journey

Let us not perish but be restored to life again

with the blessed water of regeneration

Angels of Pisces

1 ... Lachiel: A man and a woman facing one another and holding hands.

2 ... Neliel: A chest floating upon the sea.

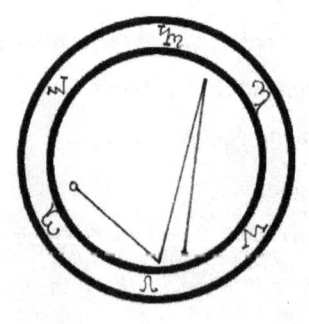

3 ... Sanael: A boar's head upon a dish.

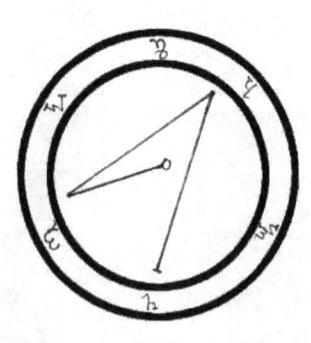

4 ... Gnasiel: A trilithon of two pillars and a lintel, a gate is set within.

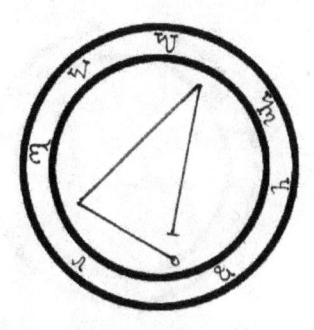

5 ... Pangael: Three men with arms linked in friendship.

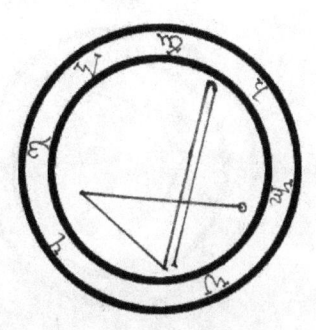

6 ... Tzapheal: A wrecked ship upon a quiet sea.

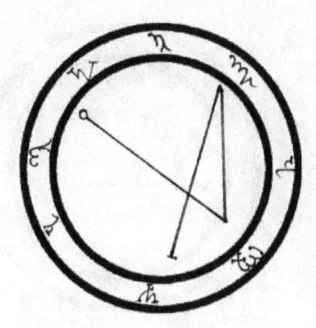

7 ... Kphiel: A book and lamp set upon a shelf in a wall.

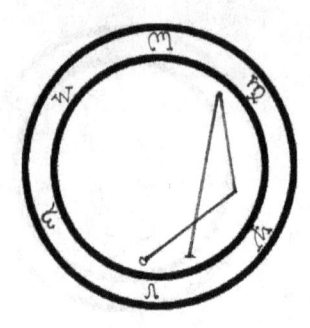

8 ... Ratziel: A man submerged in the water, his arms upraised.

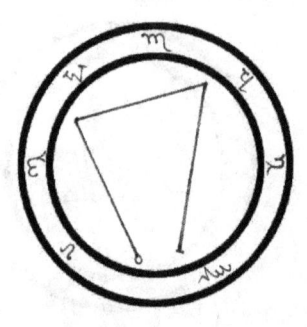

9 ... Tarajah: A man walking downhill, with a backpack and staff.

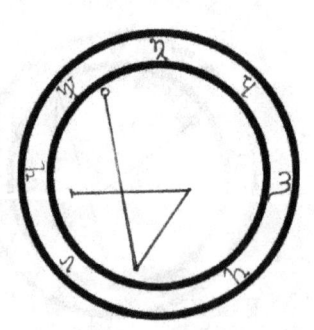

10 ... Gnathiel: A crucible, retort and mortar and pestle on a table.

11 ... Bengiel: A horse jumping a fence.

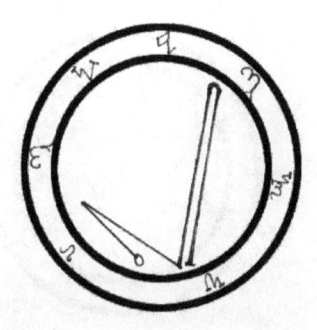

12 ... Gebiel: A truncated cone.

13 ... Dagiel: A circle within a circle.

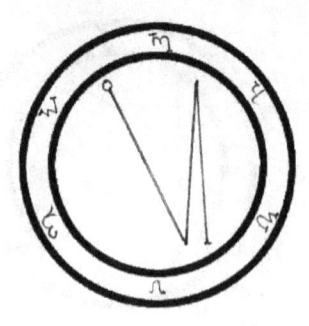

14 ... Hadiel: A man stripped to the waist and cutting logs.

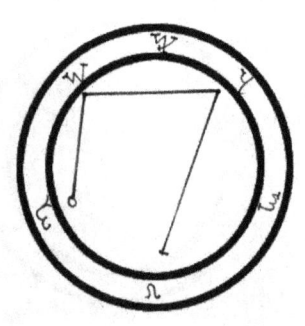

15 ... Vahajah: An arrow flying through a cloud of smoke.

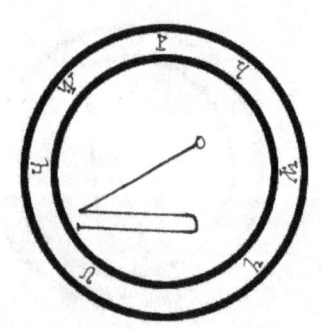

16 ... Zavael: A tiger guarding its cubs.

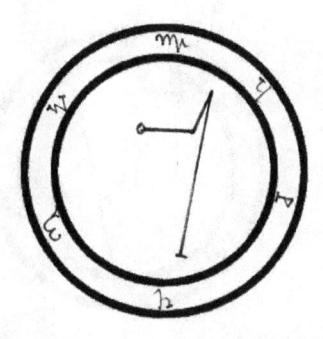

17 ... Chazael: A man falling between the timbers of a broken bridge.

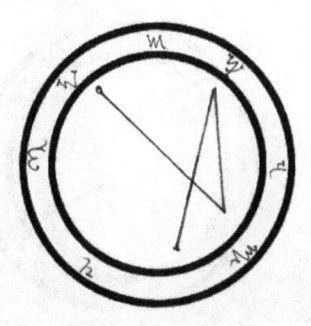

18 ... Tachael: A horse and rider falling at a fence.

19 ... Jatael: Two crossed daggers.

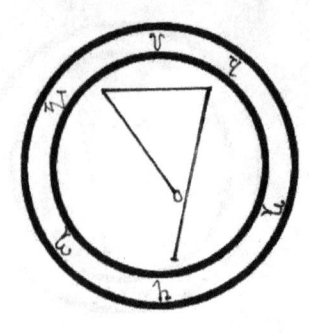

20 ... Cajaiel: A helical scroll.

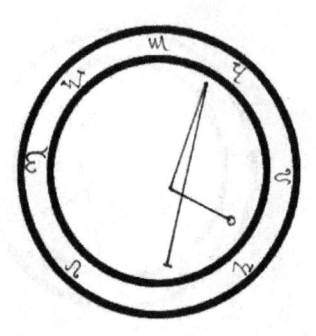

21 ... Bachiel: A new moon emerging from a cloud as lightning flashes.

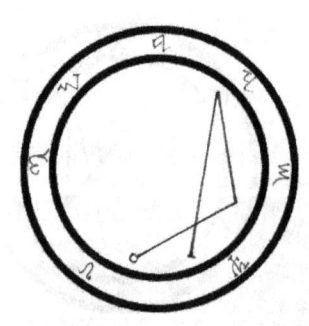

22 ... Gabiel: A dark woman standing over a prostrate man.

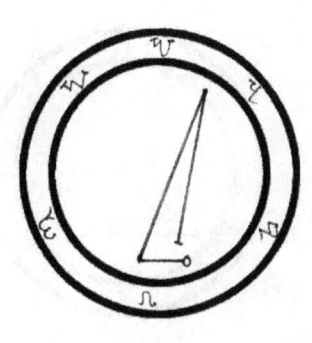

23 ... Dagiel: An archer drawing a bow.

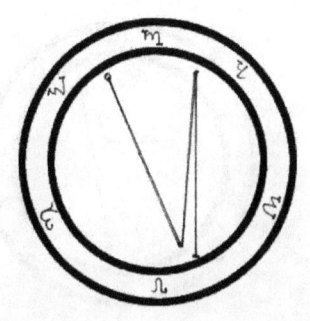

24 ... Hediel: A scantily-clad woman lying upon a couch.

25 ... Vahejah: A crown through which is set an upright sword.

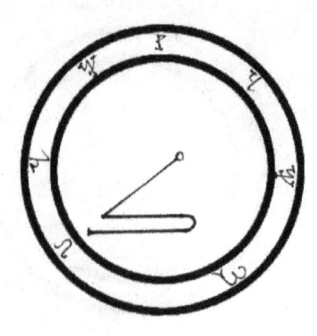

26 ... Zavael: A man in armour bearing a shield.

27 ... Chazael: An earthquake.

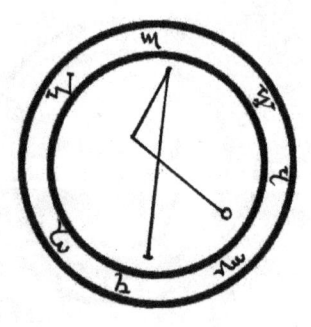

28 ... Tachiel: A serpent in a circle of fire.

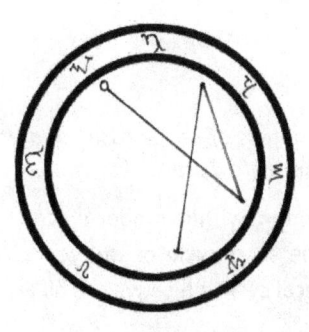

29 ... Jatael: A man adrift upon a raft floating on the sea.

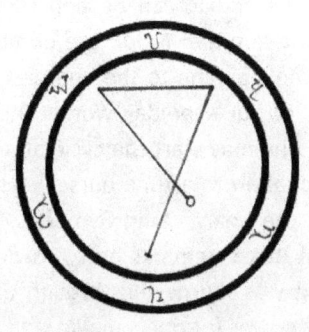

30 ... Cajael: A straight column with square top and solid base.

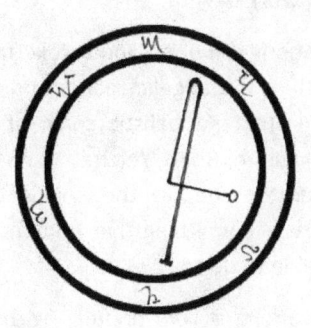

CHAPTER THREE

Praxis

> *'...let the angels of peace assist and protect this holy place, let all discord and strife depart....'*

Whilst it is common within modern occult groups of one hue or another to follow the solar cycle of the year, little has been expressed concerning the zodiacal cycle which we are all also subject to.

This work offers a means to connect with this cycle and to embrace its mysteries as they manifest in the world.

Working with the Zodiac

The energies of the zodiac can be approached by meditation and pathworking when the Sun and Moon are domiciled in their sign. This will help to attune one's psyche to the energies of the divine which are behind the activities of our everyday world. Thus, for example, starting with Aries (although one may start the cycle at any point), we can create a basic ritual or meditation to attune ourselves to and follow the Sun in its journey through the year. John Symonds, writing in the Crowley biography 'The Great Beast' remarks how Crowley was keen on zodiacal rituals when the Sun was journeying through each sign as a means to generate a source of power for one's magic, and this approach has much to commend it, as it can build a reservoir of energy within the psyche of the individual. Simple meditations on the zodiacal attributes will be found useful, particularly when they are performed after invocations of the sign that is being worked with.

With such invocations call upon and invoke the God Name first, then the Archangel and then the angelic realm, and finally the name of the sign. This follows a strict Kabbalistic chain of command through the hierarchies.... From Atziluth, Briah, Yetzirah to Assiah. Invocations can be created by the operator and, as the angels told Sir Edward Kelley, creating invocations was something that humans were created to do, as the angelic weren't able to do so.

The art of pathworking is very popular in the modern occult world, although when considering pre-Golden Dawn magic, by and large our occult forebears seemed to have not bothered with the practice. One could not however say it was completely ignored, as can be seen with some of the spiritual exercises of St Ignatius Loyola. Within his system of catholic meditations, he advocated the meditative use of biblical imagery from the life of Christ; today the magical fraternity would consider these to be path-workings. Later, Jung, the eminent Swiss psychologist, developed a similar concept and used it with his patients. There are various approaches to the arte of pathworking, a common method is whereby one is read a descriptive scene, and one immerses oneself within its imagery as it is being read out; this is a popular method within a group setting.

Or one can use a symbol and visualise it upon a door, and, with the aid of one's visualising faculties, enter the scene. The latter method, I feel, is to be preferred, as one is having an individual experience rather than a shared one, one which has been created by someone else, as in the former approach; although it does have its merits under certain circumstances. By using the symbol as a doorway, the experiences and imagery that arise, and with which one interacts, are yours alone. As they are stimulated by the working and will arise from the depth of one's being, they will be highly personal. This doesn't mean that two people cannot have a similar, or indeed the same experience, particularly when they are individuals in tune with one another, as can occur with long-standing magical groups and partners.

This in itself can often amplify any workings and can create a powerful magical reservoir which will help to empower one's magic generally. Such aids as colour and incense will also add to the ambience of the work and these will, in turn, aid in the creation of an atmosphere conducive to success. By creating an emotional link with the work, a beneficial flow of energies can be created, but this may take time as the links must be forged and worked with regularly for this to happen.

The Angels of the Zodiac

As there are twelve houses in one's natal chart there will be twelve angels who will aid the individual in the respective areas of one's life in which they are relevant. The angel who governs the degree on which the natal ascendant rises, the beginning of the first house, is considered to be the 'Lesser Guardian Angel', and by working with this angel you will gain a valued ally in life. Each angel has a descriptive sentence associated with them and these images can be simply built up in the mind under ritual conditions and experience.

The imagery presented here was used in a south Shropshire coven, to which I belonged in the 1970's. It was first used by the Welsh border conjuror John Thomas, also known as Charubel. Having abandoned his Methodist ministry Charubel created a pre-Golden Dawn occult order known as The Celestial Brotherhood, which as far as I'm aware is no longer in existence.

Meditation

Soft lighting and incense will help set the right atmosphere, as will lighting a candle, particularly one of the appropriate colour. An invocation of the zodiacal energy you are working with for aid in understanding the mystery of the sign will also help with the creation of an empathetic state of mind. Having got comfortable and regulated one's breathing, still the mind and proceed with your contemplation and workings.

Such simplified methods as these will often allow for insights into the subject under consideration, which may not have been apparent previously, but which are a useful means of ingress into their mysteries.

Pathworking

Under ritual conditions, and on getting into the right frame of mind, the individual can create a scene in their mind's eye and endeavour to place their consciousness therein and let the energies manifest accordingly. Closing down after the working will be needed to close the doors between the seen and the unseen worlds. Often questions can be answered in such workings but not always as one would wish them to be. Often the answer can come through in a feeling or a sense of what is; sometimes conversations may occur with figures who manifest, however these must be tested to see that they are who they are saying they are. To do this, use the God and Archangel names to which they will be subject; they will disappear if they are not who they claim to be, such as the angel in question. Do not worry that you will get lost at this level of working as the everyday is not far away.

Candle Magic

This can be a simple form of magic such as the lighting of a candle and the stating of one's intent; or it can be performed under ritual conditions. The consecration of the candle to a particular angel who you wish to work with is a simple matter. Drawing their seal and standing the candle on it, (safely) whilst petitioning the angel for aid can often bring surprising results; particularly if you have contacted the angel previously in meditation or via pathworking. The candle must be one that has never been used before. The ritual can be repeated for three days or as a novena over nine days. This repetition will assist the magic to manifest, particularly on more difficult problems: repetition can often work wonders.

Conjuration

Although this can be a more spectacular working, it is also one of the more demanding occult artes, and will require an experienced individual who has a deeper understanding of our arte to successfully perform this work. It will also require some astrological knowledge as you will need to work when the moon is traversing the angel's degree of the zodiac. The gathering of one's magical equipment and a shewstone will be necessary and I have written in depth elsewhere about such items of magical regalia, and would refer you to previous works for any information you may require. Working at this level is demanding and the individual will have to isolate themselves as far as practical from the distractions of the everyday world around them as they focus their will upon the successful outcome of the working. This can be achieved through regular meditation upon the working and a strict regime of purification, with no or little contact with the outside world until the working has been performed.

Conjuration into the shewstone will allow the individual to create real links with the angel that cannot be dismissed as illusionary, particularly when results manifest in one's life. For some, this level of working will be suitable as they have the intent necessary for this work, however candle magic and the consecration of the angelic seal will also bring events to pass within one's life. So, one may ask - why bother with arduous workings when simplified approaches will work too? This is true but for some, who have the mindset to approach the angelic realms at this level, it will be like climbing mountains 'because they're there.'

Talismans

These are useful occult aids and a consecrated talisman will make contact with the angel easier, particularly if it is worked with regularly.

For example, once the seal is consecrated, when the moon is passing over the degree of the zodiac which is attributed to the angel in question, one can burn a little incense and light a candle which can be placed upon the talisman, or the talisman be held in the rising incense smoke as the angel is invoked. As time goes by such actions will feed the talisman and it will become more active. Talismans can be drawn upon parchment or paper in the colours of the angel, for example the angels of Aries will need to be drawn in red inks, the others according to their zodiacal colours. Carving the seal upon a gemstone associated with the sign is good, more so as you could then wear it as a ring and it will be active within your aura. This approach would be useful when connecting with the angel who rules your ascendant.

Rituals

Using Aries as our example, I give three magical workings as templates which can be easily adapted for working with other signs. All ritual practices and operations given can be found in my other published works. Whilst I have given some invocations in Latin the English equivalent can be used as an alternative should you prefer.

Pathworking

- Lesser Banishing Ritual of the Pentagram or similar
- Prayer to the Highest
- Invocation of Zodiac energies
- Visualising the doorway and the projection of one's consciousness
- Return
- Close
- Light a red candle and burn Dragon's Blood as incense
- Perform LBRP

- Prayer

    Thou who art beyond all things

    We thee invoke

    Aid us with this our holy work

    Which we perform in thy name...

- Invocation

    Trace astrological sign in the air before you and say....

    I invoke O Holy Ram by the might of the divine name YHVH

    And by the Holy Archangel Malkidiel

    That the Holy Angel of Aries Shariel grants us ingress unto thy holy realms....

    Share with us the mysteries of thy being

    for we too are servants of the God Most High

- Intone the following invocation unto the energies of the Celestial Ram...

    Tu es ille Aries catli claaustra refringere

    Iubet et nos in viam

    nostrum vitam activam

    cor nostrum impleatur animo

    perseverare invictam ut vitae viam nostrum.

Now sitting comfortably and relaxed, let the mind empty of everyday concerns and let your breathing become even. As the mind clears, visualise a door before you on which the sign of Aries is drawn in red, imagine you are walking into the door and the realms beyond.

It is considered magical courtesy not to speak to anyone until they speak to you first. Invoke the name of God and the Archangel too as a test of any figures who may appear, if they do not belong they will disappear. After your experience come back through the door and shut it firmly as being symbolic of the closure of the means of ingress and egress between the worlds.

Give thanks to the holy names that you have invoked and the energies of Aries for sharing with you something of their mysteries.

Close with LBRP.

This method can also be used to contact one of the angels of your chart by using the imagery of their name, as given. Simply visualise the scene and walk into it; usual protocols apply. Whilst this may seem a simple method, regular working will make contact easier.

Candle Magic Ritual

- LBRP
- Invocation of the Highest
- Invocation of Zodiacal energies
- Consecration and dedication of the Zodiacal candle
- Light candle and visualise clearly the outcome as you state what it is that you want to happen
- Give thanks and close the ritual

The first three points have been covered above, although after performing LBRP the compass points may be opened as our arte demands. State the purpose of the ritual; this must be clear and unambiguous, with no doubts as to the successful outcome of the magic that is being worked.

Doubt can be fatal for one's magic, so do not indulge!

Remember, 'As I Do Will… So Mote It Be!'

The candle is now sprinkled with holy water as means to banish the past and words to this effect are pronounced.

'In the Name of the God Most High

Let all malignancy and hindrance be cast forth hence from

So that my will may manifest.'

Inscribe on the candle the seal and name of the angel who you are petitioning for help, and then hold the candle in the rising incense smoke while you declare your intent. As you gaze upon the candle see in your mind's eye the image which is associated with the angel who you are working with, this is your call to the unseen worlds, and you may be sure that it will be answered.

If you can phrase this in rhyming couplets so much the better as the deeps of your mind will pick up the intention more easily.

For example:

> *'Hear Me O Angel (name) for this I say*
>
> *For thine aid I invoke in every way*
>
> *Hear my words which I address to thee*
>
> *For This My Will So Mote It Be!*

(State Intent Clearly)

Take a vial of consecrated oil and starting in the middle of the candle rub some of the oil on it. By starting in the middle of the candle and working towards the end and then repeating the action towards the other end your intent is becoming focused as you perform this action. See your will coming to fruition as you do this.

Call upon the angel to aid you as you light the candle, and gaze into the flame as it burns. See the outcome forming and let it burn out completely as the energies are released.

Give thanks to the angel and the energies that you have invoked and declare the rite has ended.

Talismans

- LBRP
- Opening of the Compass Points
- Invocations to the Highest
- Invocation of the Energies of the sign which the angel belongs to
- Consecration and empowering of the talisman
- Give thanks
- Close the ritual

The first three points have been covered previously. The seal of the angel is to be drawn upon the talisman, it can be etched on the relevant planetary metal, or inscribed on the zodiacal gemstone, or it can be drawn in ink on parchment or good paper. If you do this try to use ink of the appropriate colour i.e. for angels of Aries use red ink. The best time for the ritual will be when the moon is on the same degree of the zodiac as the angel you are working with, failing that let it be in the same sign as the angel. If you are familiar with astrology then one may consider working when the moon is either sextile, 60° (from the angel's degree, either side) or trine (120°) with the angel's zodiacal degree. These are also strong positions for our working.

With the invocation of the angel remember the formula that calls upon the God Name then the Archangel and then the angel. Using the angel of the first degree of Aries as our example one can proceed thus...

> 'For in and by the Holy Name of God YHVH
>
> I invoke the Holy Archangel of Aries... Malkidiel
>
> That the Mighty Angel Biael may ..... (state purpose of the working)
>
> Thou who art the angel of the first degree of Aries
>
> For by the Holy and the Mighty Names of God
>
> I invoke thine aid that this talisman... (again state intention)
>
> According unto my holy will'

As with the consecration of the candle previously, the talisman is sprinkled with holy water saying as one does so

> 'For in and by the names of God
>
> Let all malignancy and hindrance be cast out from
>
> So that the power of (state angel's name) may enter herein according unto my holy will'

Hold the talisman in the rising incense and invoke the angel via the names of God and the Archangel, and as you do so see the imagery of the angel gather around, and in, the talisman that you hold. See the energy concentrate and let the talisman soak it up like a sponge does water. As it does so, the energies become more concentrated in the talisman until they appear as a fiery ball of the colour of the energy. With this being a talisman of the first angel of Aries this will be bright red.

Take the talisman to the east and hold upon high, stating that it is en-hallowed according unto thy will... do this at the southern, western and northern quarters too. Give thanks to the energies invoked and declare the rite is over thus....

> 'I give thanks to the Most Holy Name of God YHVH
>
> And to the Mighty Archangel of Aries Malkidiel
>
> And to the Holy Angel Biael, angel of the first degree of Aries
>
> For aiding me with this my most holy work.'

Whilst LBRP can be performed it will not be necessary at this point as a simple release will suffice....

'I now set free any spirits en-trapped by this ceremony

Go in peace to your abodes and habitations

And may the blessings of the God Most High be upon us and about us all now and for always.'

Every month when the moon travels over the angel's zodiacal degree the talisman can be held in incense smoke as you visualise the angel's imagery forming in and around it. By doing this you will enable the talisman to keep working for you as the energies are being recharged regularly.

- Conjuration of the angel
- Preparation
- LBRP or similar
- Opening of the Compass Points
- State intent
- Consecration of the seal of the angel
- Prayers for success
- Call unto the angel
- Reception of angel
- Close

This demanding work will require the operator to isolate themselves from much of the daily trivia which assails our lives with regular monotony. The world of facebook, banal conversations, and the many and varied pointless interactions with other people, all these and others must be avoided or at least kept to a strict minimum for several days as the conjuror gets into the 'right frame of mind' to receive the angel.

A strict regime of no alcohol, sexual activity and purity in both body and mind will need to be developed. Remember what the angels told Sir Edward Kelley: *'Long may he knock who is filthily attired.'*

Thus, the angels expect you to be purified and in the right mindset, consequently these strictures will put this level of working beyond most people as they will not wish to be subject to such demands; more so if they can get a result another way. But the arte demands effort and such efforts become our sacrifice which we make as we prepare for our working.

For seven days, three at the very least, restrict all social activity and contact with people, consume a simple diet free of animal flesh. Wash daily and pour consecrated water over one's head afterwards, so a bath or shower will be best for this. Wear a white robe and enter the temple or work space, recite prayers of your own devising for success. It will useful to also meditate on the angel's imagery as well. Perform this operation in the morning and in the evening.

Burning a little of the incense relating to the angel's sign will help set the mood. Prepare an altar with a clean cloth of the right colour; as we are still working with the example or template of the angel of the first degree of Aries, I will stay with them. Therefore, in this case the altar cloth will be red, the candles, however, will be white and unused. These will need to be consecrated, as will the incense and the charcoal upon which it will be burnt. The seal of the angel will be consecrated and placed under the shewstone.

Prayers for success are given and the conjuration recited and the shewstone watched, sometimes the angel may make their presence apparent sooner rather than later. However, the conjuration may need to be recited three times or so before your patience is rewarded, and the angel may not appear in the way you may expect them to do so. Indeed, there may only be a sense of a presence in the shewstone and not a clearly defined figure. But regardless of how they manifest you will know when they are there. Requests and petitions should then be stated, and you should also arrange that a sign will be given when the energies are released. The late Michael Howard told me this was referred to by his teacher Madeline Montalban as 'Checks on Earth.'

Often with magical workings there will be a series of coincidental events related to the working as the current is manifesting; these are a good sign and should be welcomed.

Having placed the consecrated seal of the angel under the shewstone, which is on the altar and with the Compass Points now opened, invoke God for success in this holy work. Facing east recite the conjuration....

> 'O Thou Great and Mighty Angel (name of Angel)
>
> Who governeth the degree of (state where in the zodiac)
>
> Under the Holy Name of God (state God Name)
>
> And the Archangel.....
>
> (name of Archangel of the particular zodiacal sign)
>
> I do entreat thee to appear now here before me
>
> in this shewstone of the arte.

> *For I who art a servant of the same thy God do in his Holy Name*
>
> *Conjure and invoke thee to make manifest according*
>
> *to my holy will.*
>
> *For I invoke thee in the Name of God that thou come forth from thy abodes and habitations.*
>
> *For thou O mighty angel of (state degree of zodiac)*
>
> *Who art placed within thine office by him who made us all, in his name I do conjure thee and invoke unto this shewstone of the arte here before me on this altar speaking words of truth and understanding.*
>
> *Hear Me! O Angel (state name) Hear Me!*
>
> *Be thou friendly unto me!*
>
> *Aid me!*
>
> *Assist me in mine endeavours!*
>
> *Come now make manifest as I do will!*
>
> *For I too am a servant of the God Most High!'*

Wait and watch... do not strain but hold the mind blank and wait for the angel to acknowledge your words... If nothing is happening then repeat the conjuration again. When the angel's presence is apparent one may ask what it is that you wish, providing it is in their office.

Therefore, if it is a matter concerning your health, for example, then it will be the angel who rules that degree of your natal chart where your sixth house of health matters arises, and so on.

When the energies are fading thank the angel and the Names of God and the Archangel....

> *'For I do thank thee O Holy Angel... (name)*
>
> *for aiding me with mine endeavours*
>
> *For I give thanks also unto the Mighty Name of God (God Name)*
>
> *and the Holy Archangel (Archangel Name)*
>
> *for assisting me in this my holy will.*

Therefore, let there be grace, peace and harmony between me and thee now and for always...

So Mote It Be!'

Take a few moments to let the atmosphere settle and depart.

Whilst this is a simplified account of such workings it is potent nonetheless and can be adapted and amended accordingly....

And as the angels said to Sir Edward and Dr John Dee...

'For God hath given up to thee the keys to his storehouse.

Enter therein but wisely.'

Index

A

Advakiel 110
Agrippa 12, 13
Ambriel 44
Amnitziel 143
Angelus 14
Apuleius 13
Aquarius 21, 132, 133
Araziel 33
Aries 19, 21, 22, 23, 154, 158, 159, 161, 162, 164
Asmodel 33

B

Barkiel 99
Benedictine 12

C

Cancer 21, 55, 56
Capricorn 21, 121, 122
Charubel 13, 156
Chedeqiel 88
Crowley 154

F

Ficino 13

G

Gemini 21, 44, 45
Golden Dawn 15, 16, 154, 156
Greek Magical Papyri 15

H

Hamaliel 77
Hanael 121
Hermes Trismegistus 13
HHVY 21, 77, 143
Hollandus 5

HVHY 21, 55
HVYH 21, 66
HYHV 21, 121
HYVH 21, 132

J

Jung 155
Junius 5
Jupiter 110, 143

K

Kabbalah 5, 13
Kambriel 132
kamea 14
Kelley 154, 163

L

Leo 21, 66, 67
Lesser Key of Solomon 11
Libra 14, 21, 88, 89
Libra, ... 14
Lilly 21
Loyola 155
Luna 55

M

Malkidiel 22, 159, 162
Mars 17, 22, 99
Medici 11
Mercury 44, 77
Middle Pillar 16
Mirandola 13
moon ... 16, 32, 62, 73, 103, 114, 150, 154, 157, 158, 161, 163
Muriel 55

N

natal chart ... 10, 19, 20, 21, 155, 165

Neoplatonism 13

O

Ovid 13

P

Pakiel 55
Paracelsus 5, 11, 12, 13
Pauline Arte 10
Pisces 21, 143, 144
Pliny the Elder 13

R

Regardie 5, 15
Reuchlin 13
Rosicrucian 11

S

Sagittarius 21, 110, 111
Saitzel 99
Sameqiel 121
Sarayel 44
Saritiel 110
Saturn 121, 132
Scorpio 21, 99, 100
Sharatiel 66
Sharhiel 22
Shelathiel 77
shewstone 157, 164, 165
Steganographia 11

Sun 16, 19, 20, 66, 67, 71, 72, 106, 154

T

talisman 158, 161, 162, 163
Taurus 14, 21, 33, 34
Tetragrammaton 10
Theurgia Goetia 11, 169
Trithemius 11, 12, 13
Turner 10, 11
Tzakmiqiel 132

V

Vakabiel 143
Venus 14, 33, 88
Verkiel 66
VHHY 21, 99
VHYH 21, 88
Virgil 13
Virgo 21, 77, 78
Von Heidenberg 12
VYHH 21, 110

Y

YHHV 21, 33
YHVH 21, 22, 159, 162
YVHH 21, 44

Z

Zuriel 88

Gary St. Michael Nottingham

Other Books by this Author:

Foundations of Practical Sorcery, 2015
- Vol. I – Liber Noctis
- Vol. II – Ars Salomonis
- Vol. III – Ars Geomantica
- Vol. IV – Ars Theurgia Goetia
- Vol. V – Otz Chim
- Vol. VI – Ars Speculum
- Vol. VII – Liber Terriblis

Ars Alchemica: Foundations of Practical Alchemy, 2016

Welsh Border Witchcraft: A rendition of the Occult History of the Welsh March, 2018

Visit: www.avaloniabooks.co.uk for more information